To my wife Amanda and daughter Tessa, for untold love and inspiration.

The
Practical Media
Dictionary
Jeremy Orlebar

The Practical Media Dictionary

Jeremy Orlebar

LEARNING RESOURCES CENTRE

Havering College
of Further and Higher Education

ARNOLD

302.2303 A9

31356

First published in Great Britain in 2003 by
Arnold, a member of the Hodder Headline Group,
338 Euston Road, London NW1 3BH

http://www.arnoldpublishers.com

Distributed in the United States of America by
Oxford University Press Inc.,
198 Madison Avenue, New York, NY 10016

© 2003 Jeremy Orlebar

All rights reserved. No part of this publication may be reproduced or
transmitted in any form or by any means, electronically or mechanically,
including photocopying, recording or any information storage or retrieval
system, without either prior permission in writing from the publisher or a
licence permitting restricted copying. In the United Kingdom such licences
are issued by the Copyright Licensing Agency: 90 Tottenham Court Road,
London W1T 4LP.

The advice and information in this book are believed to be true and
accurate at the date of going to press, but neither the author[s] nor the publisher
can accept any legal responsibility or liability for any errors or omissions.

British Library Cataloguing in Publication Data
A catalogue record for this book is available from the British Library

Library of Congress Cataloging-in-Publication Data
A catalog record for this book is available from the Library of Congress

ISBN 0 340 809035 (hb)
ISBN 0 340 809043 (pb)

1 2 3 4 5 6 7 8 9 10

Typeset in 9/11.5 Baskerville Book by Phoenix Photosetting, Chatham, Kent
Printed and bound in Great Britain by MPG Books Ltd, Bodmin, Cornwall

What do you think about this book? Or any other Arnold title?
Please send your comments to feedback.arnold@hodder.co.uk

ACKNOWLEDGEMENTS

The author would like to thank the kind people who helped bring this publication to fruition. Michael Turner, for contributing so many good photographs. The many students from Farnborough College of Technology, and elsewhere, who agreed to be photographed while working on their projects. Richie at VMI, for kindly supplying action photographs. Lesley Riddle at Arnold, for so much good-humoured advice.

The media industry covers an extensive range of activities, jobs, organisations, companies, equipment and new developments associated with creating broadcast television, radio, film, video, print publications, and new digital and interactive media. There is a great deal of specialist language and jargon, and many media-specific definitions used in all these areas. The difficulty for students embarking on any media or multimedia course, or for new entrants to the industry, is how to get up to speed. Not only is there a lot of new information to absorb, but no single book covers the language of the film crew as well as that of multimedia. This is an industry whose parts are converging. Students need to be able to communicate across the different areas, skills and methods typically understood in the industry.

The Practical Media Dictionary aims to define and explain a comprehensive selection of the most commonly used vocabulary of practical media production throughout the industry. It encompasses the everyday language, the most encountered phrases, typical job definitions, relevant organisations and institutions, most utilised equipment and much of the commonly employed technical jargon associated with practical activities. More importantly, it attempts to demystify the language and idiom used right across the media. This includes a whole range of processes, jobs, skills and associated working practices.

Each entry tries not only to define and explain, but also to develop further understanding. It may be a piece of equipment such as a **SOUND MIXING DESK** or a **DIGITAL BETACAM**, or an activity such as creating a filming schedule. After each definition there is accessible text explaining more about what the equipment does or what the activity involves, and, if appropriate, how and why. An entry may be an explanation of one of the many production or technical jobs found in the media, such as **RUNNER** or **ASSISTANT CAMERAMAN**. The role and nature of the job is fully explained. Organisations and associations that people working in the media are likely to come across are also included, along with their website addresses.

The dictionary aims to be a companion that can be referred to again and again, with easy-to-read, clear and uncluttered definitions. Under each heading there are clearly identified links to related entries. Only a few ubiquitous and easily understood words are not identified, although there are entries for each one. These are: camera, film, internet, software, television and radio. Photographs and illustrations offer further information, enhancing a range of entries.

Virtually all media and multimedia educational courses have elements of practical work. This can range from creating a poster with a desktop publishing package to making an animated film, working with computer-generated graphics or producing a sophisticated drama on digital video. The day-to-day working language, the customised roles, the specific deployment of skills and specialist activities in a practical media environment can at first be daunting. This dictionary aims to smooth the pathway into practical media production. It demystifies the commonly used language and industry-specific vocabulary, develops knowledge, increases confidence and helps the student understand the way practical media works.

1

ACTION   The instruction used on a TV or movie set to inform the actors and **CREW** that the camera is rolling, and now is the time to start the action. Used to start a scene or go from a predetermined and agreed point in the script. Usually given by the **DIRECTOR** or assistant director (**AD**). Action also refers to any activity on screen. An action movie indicates plenty of physical activity, including fights, daring stunts and exciting car chases.

ACTUALITY   **SOUND** recorded on location for a radio programme that is not an **INTERVIEW**. This sound may be **BACKGROUND** sound that can be used later as a separate track in the edit – see **ATMOS** – or it can be a collection of sounds from the **LOCATION** recording. Often used to make a radio report more 'interesting'.

AD   Assistant Director. On a film or television drama there can be three or more assistant directors who work to the **DIRECTOR**. The First AD is the director's most trusted and closest helper, making sure everything on the set is exactly as the director has requested and calling for silence before the action begins. The Second AD typically works with the actors and prepares **EXTRAS** for their role in a scene, and works ahead on the next day's shoot. The Third AD helps the Second, and deals with crowd scenes and controlling the public. May help with preparing schedules and setting up scenes.

AD LIB   The words of a **PRESENTER** or **CONTRIBUTOR** to a radio or TV programme that are not scripted. Refers to when contributors are asked to talk about a subject in an unrestricted way, with no reference to a **SCRIPT**.

ADOBE PREMIERE   www.adobe.com Trade name of popular and widely used software for desktop computer **NON-LINEAR EDITING**. Available for Mac- or Windows-based computers. Video **RUSHES** are loaded onto the computer **HARD DISK** via **FIREWIRE** by choosing movie capture or **BATCH DIGITISING**. The **SOUND** and pictures of the rushes can then be viewed and edited on the **TIMELINE**. Version 6 onwards has a large array of visual effects and **TRANSITIONS** with more than enough **AUDIO** tracks. To view transitions the selected **FRAMES** have to be **RENDERED**. Compatible with other Adobe packages including **PHOTOSHOP** and After Effects – a highly regarded software for creating **SPECIAL EFFECTS**. On Premiere, **TITLES** and end **CREDITS** can be created easily and added to the timeline. Depending on computer power and the data storage capacity, long sequences or whole programmes can be edited and rendered up to broadcast standard. *See **AVID**, **Final Cut Pro**.*

ADSL   Asymmetric Digital Subscriber Line. Refers to a fast internet connection line. Used in place of a traditional telephone line with an upgraded modem. Offers quicker access to the

Editing on Adobe Premiere

internet, with increased services such as reasonable-quality pictures with video STREAMING. *See Broadband.*

AFM   Assistant Floor Manager. In a TV STUDIO the AFM works to the FLOOR MANAGER and has headphones to hear TALKBACK with the GALLERY. Among a variety of duties, collects guests and actors from the dressing rooms and the GREEN ROOM. Good training to become a floor manager.

AFVPA   Advertising, Film and Videotape Producers' Association, 26 Noel Street, London W1V 3RD www.afvpa.com The association that represents the interests of producers of television and film commercials.

AM   Radio/audio. Amplitude Modulation. Usually found as a radio transmission system where the amplitude, or value, of the carrier signal is varied according to the amplitude of the audio signal. Broadly speaking, as the music changes the signal carrier changes too. In radio, AM is often known as 'crackly old Medium Wave'. *See FM.*

AMBIENT SOUND   The natural background SOUND that can be picked up by a MICROPHONE in a STUDIO or any LOCATION. This is the background sound of the production area without any **DIALOGUE** or any other production activity taking place. Used as background sound to a dialogue recording that is laid under the whole scene to give a sense of aural continuity. Recorded by the sound **RECORDIST** to use in the sound **DUB** in **POST-PRODUCTION**. *See Audio, Audio Mixer.*

AMPLIFIER   Equipment for increasing the strength of an electrical signal. In order to hear music or speech from a **CD** player on a loudspeaker, an amplifier has to increase the electrical signal sufficiently to drive the speaker.

ANALOGUE   A representation in electrical values of something that is a physical quantity. For example, a singer sings into a **MICROPHONE**. The microphone converts the changes in air pressure created by **SOUND** waves from the singer into electrical signals. The continuously variable sound waves are directly represented with corresponding variable electrical values by an AC voltage from the microphone. There is a direct relationship between the pattern of the sound waves and the electrical pattern. The recorded electrical signals are analogous to the singer's sound vibrations. A record deck with a turntable to play vinyl records is using an analogue system. The turntable rotates the record, a stylus tracks the grooves in the record and converts them to electrical signals. **DIGITAL** systems, which are less prone to error and more compact, are taking over the recording of audio and visual material. Analogue systems are still used for home and some low-end professional recording, e.g. the recording of pictures onto magnetic **VIDEOTAPE** by **VHS**. All pictures and sound were recorded by analogue systems until the advent of **DIGITAL RECORDING**.

ANAMORPHIC   Literally means a distorted image that, when viewed correctly, returns to normal. On a TV camera, an anamorphic lens is used to squeeze or compress a **WIDESCREEN** (16:9) image into a standard 4:3 **FORMAT**. For transmission, this is unsqueezed to show the original widescreen (16:9) format. Broadcasting companies require programmes to be made in widescreen, and a standard camera can be converted to do this by using an anamorphic lens adaptor. Check it is a true 16:9 conversion lens.

ANCHOR   The television **PRESENTER**, generally but not always in the **TV STUDIO**, who is the main link person in a magazine-style news or factual TV programme.

ANGLE   Print. In a news article, the angle is the main point featured in the article and the way the article unfolds this point. Each paper will have a different angle on a story. In moving image production, the angle is the line along which a camera looks at a subject. This relates to where the camera is positioned. *See High-Angle Shot, Low-Angle Shot, Wide Angle.*

ANIMATION   Still images that can be combined to produce the illusion of moving images. Drawings or models are filmed or videoed frame by frame. Cartoon or 'cell' animation involves drawing separate images onto transparent sheets or cells. A character appears to move as each cell progresses the action to a small degree. Between twelve and twenty-five drawings are required for every second of screen time. When projected at the normal speed, the viewer sees continuous movement. The process has taken on a new lease of life in movies (for example, *The Lord of the Rings* or *Shrek*) with computer-generated animation (**CGA**) where 3D images are created on computer and the animation process is digitised. Computer-generated images can be combined with **LIVE ACTION** to produce incredible effects. All but the most simple animation is expensive to produce and very labour intensive. For a TV series, costs of £9000 a minute are not unusual, but animation is very popular globally as it can be dubbed into other languages easily. Just think of the worldwide success of *The Simpsons*. Animation is used in many areas, e.g. commercials, computer games, music promos, children's programmes, **MULTIMEDIA**, comedy and feature films. *See Stop-Frame Animation.*

ANIMATION WORLD NETWORK   www.awn.com Large animation-related publishing group on the internet. Provides relevant and helpful information about all aspects of animation, covering areas as diverse as animator profiles, independent film distribution, commercial studio activities, computer-generated imaging (**CGI**) and other animation technologies, as well as in-depth coverage of current events in all fields of animation. Has a recruiting section with free postings and access to recruitment advertisements. Comprehensive animation school and college database for researching and finding information on over 400 animation education courses in 34 different countries.

ANSWER PRINT   Film. The first print of an edited film to come back from the **LABS** after **NEG CUTTING**. This is a **GRADED PRINT** but may need some revisions to the grading or to some of the optical effects to be fully satisfactory. The **EDITOR** has to minutely check the answer print for anything that is unsatisfactory, such as negative cutting errors. The 'answers' will go back to the labs with the print and then returned as a second answer print. This will continue until the film is deemed perfect or time runs out.

APERTURE   Controls the amount of light that enters a camera. The aperture is the opening through which light passes into a camera. The **IRIS** – a system of interlocking metal leaves that can be opened and closed to expand or contract the space – controls the size of the aperture. Aperture controls the **DEPTH OF FIELD**.

ARCHIVE   Film, video or sound recordings that are held in an archive or library and can be accessed by a producer, usually for a fee.

ARMOURER   Skilled and trained person who looks after any real or replica armaments on a film set. All weapons of any sort are checked and kept safely by the armourer, and training given to actors in the use of firearms.

ARTICLE   Print. A complete, written composition by a journalist or contributor to a publication.

ARTIST'S CONTRACT   Contract issued by the broadcaster or production company to employ actors, **PRESENTERS**, musicians or other **TALENT** for a particular TV or radio programme or film. On-screen talent normally has an artist's contract.

ASA   Film. American Standard Association. A way of indicating the way **FILM STOCK** reacts to light. A low ASA, such as 50, has a finer grain and a sharper picture than film with a higher ASA of 200. A low ASA needs more light on the subject, so may be used for daylight shots. Faster film or higher ASA works better in lower light conditions, but there is a trade-off in that the film is more grainy. *See Lighting Cameraman.*

ASPECT RATIO   The ratio of height to width of a television picture or film FRAME. The international standard for shooting films to show in a cinema is 1.33:1, although many feature films are now shot in a WIDESCREEN ratio. Standard TV picture aspect ratio is 4:3, which is very similar to 1.33:1. The width (4) of the frame is longer than the height (3). Today, broadcast TV in the US and UK is shot and shown in a widescreen format. This has a generally agreed aspect ratio of 16:9 or 1.77:1. Many productions agree to 'protect' the 4:3 area in the frame by ensuring important parts of the action are within that area and make sense to viewers without widescreen TVs. (Some broadcasters also use a 14:9 version of widescreen.)

ASSEMBLE EDITING   A method of EDITING video where the editing process means the pictures and SOUND have to be assembled in the required order of the story. The selected pictures and sound are copied from the RUSHES and recorded in the chosen order onto blank VIDEOTAPE. In assemble mode, video and AUDIO tracks are transferred together, and the control TRACK is recorded with each edit and not laid down beforehand. This method of video editing is associated with LINEAR EDITING. *See Digital Editing, Editing.*

ASSEMBLY ORDER or ASSEMBLY   A list on paper, usually prepared by the DIRECTOR, of the order in which selected SHOTS and SOUND should be put together to achieve a first assembly of a TV programme or film. The in point and out point of each selected sound clip is marked with the help of a TRANSCRIPT. Chosen pictures and sound are marked with their in and out TIME CODE so that the EDITOR knows where to start and finish each shot and how long it is. Notes on size and content for each shot are usually provided to assist the editor.

ASSISTANT CAMERAMAN   Member of the film or video crew who helps the LIGHTING CAMERAMAN or the DIRECTOR OF PHOTOGRAPHY (DOP). The job entails knowledge and understanding of how a moving-image camera works. Requires skill, knowledge and operational ability such as pulling focus *(see Pull Focus)*, loading the film MAGAZINE and operating the CLAPPERBOARD. On a production using film, the first assistant cameraman helps the DOP choose the correct LENS for the SCENE and makes sure the FOCUS is kept by measuring the distance between the subject and the camera. The Second Assistant Cameraman loads the unexposed film into the camera, sends RUSHES off to the LABS and notes how much FILM STOCK has been used. *See Camera Operator, Cinematographer.*

ASSISTANT PRODUCER   On factual programmes in TV, the assistant producer works with the PRODUCER, and is often the RESEARCHER and the location director of short film INSERTS. Can be the studio director for a TV STUDIO-based programme. He or she will be involved in writing the SCRIPT, booking kit and film crews, overseeing GRAPHICS and selecting contributors as well as being involved in POST-PRODUCTION.

ASSOCIATE PRODUCER   Heavily involved with the BUDGET in a large film or TV production. Instrumental in the PRE-PRODUCTION, planning and SCHEDULING of a shoot, and in getting hold of key personnel, as well as helping to set up the whole project. Works with the PRODUCER and the production manager. *See Film Producer.*

ASTON   Brand name of an industry standard text and GRAPHICS generator used in a TV control GALLERY, and in POST-PRODUCTION facilities. Creates and manipulates graphics and

Aston caption generator

words for use in TV programmes, including **NAME SUPERS** and any text used on screen, e.g. football results.

ATMOS Background or atmospheric **SOUND** that is only just audible for a TV, film or radio **LOCATION**. There is some atmospheric **SOUND** at every location, both **INTERIOR** and **EXTERIOR**, however quiet it may seem. It is important to record this **AMBIENT SOUND** to add to the **SOUNDTRACK** of quiet or silent passages in the **SCRIPT** to maintain the sound quality of the location. Atmos or a buzz track is recorded at the place of the action by the **SOUND** recordist, usually for one minute when everyone must keep silent. Used in editing to help make the audio joins smoother. *See Ambient Sound, Dub.*

AUDIENCE Anyone who consumes or interacts with media products. Those individuals, families and groups who watch or listen to mass communication mediums such as radio and television. Originally means the act of hearing and refers to a collection of people who are within range of hearing a performance of some kind without electronic aid. Audiences for media products can be divided into mass and niche. A mass audience can be measured as a percentage of the population and is considered to be homogeneous in that it represents the whole community. Many radio and TV programmes are aimed at a niche audience. This can still be a large audience. Members of a niche audience usually have a link such as lifestyle, social class, gender, age, culture or similar interests. A programme about fishing would be aimed at a niche audience, even though fishing is an extremely popular sport. For the press and broadcasting, measuring the size of the audience is important. Advertisers need to how many people watched their commercials. TV schedulers need to know who is watching and what programmes attract the largest audiences. The press need reliable statistics on the number of readers of a publication. Different measuring systems are used for each area of the mass media. *See BARB, Prime Time, Rajar, Ratings.*

AUDIO   The name for any SOUND used in a media context. *See Sound.*

AUDIO MIXER   Electronic equipment to MIX and BALANCE sound signals from various sources. Can be a battery-driven portable with just a few channels, such as an SQN 4S audio mixer, suitable for mixing outputs from MICROPHONES while recording in the field. A large audio mixer with 24 or more sound channels in a sound recording studio is known as a SOUND MIXING DESK. *See Dub.*

AUDIO SAMPLING   Method of recording AUDIO material digitally. The SOUND waves produced, by musicians, for example, are sampled, or given a digital value, many thousands of times a second. The binary sequences created by this process can be stored on tape or disc. These can then be read by a laser in a CD player for example, reconfigured as electrical waves via a converter and then played back for listeners through a loudspeaker. *See Speaker.*

AUDITION   Meeting to interview actors or performers for a TV or radio show or film. Meeting to find suitable actors for characters in a film or drama. The DIRECTOR and/or the PRODUCER are involved in talking to hopeful actors to try and determine who will be suitable for the particular parts in the film. Most actors have a video cassette SHOW REEL with examples of their work, so they are rarely asked to actually perform in front of the director. It is often more a case of discovering if the chemistry between them is right, or whether the actor's approach to the part fits in with the director's concept of the role.

AUTOCUE   Brand name and generic term for industry standard technical prompting equipment that displays sections of the SCRIPT in front of the TV camera. The script can then be read by a PRESENTER, newsreader or an actor looking straight to camera. A screen is attached in front of the LENS of a video camera, displaying lines of script. An operator types in the text, and can control the speed, movement and size of the script, slowing down or speeding up according to how the presenter reads. Used extensively in virtually all TV STUDIO programmes, especially news and any presenter-led programmes. Any system like this is known as a TELEPROMPTER.

AUTO-EXPOSURE   Term used to describe the ability of a still, video or film camera to measure the light coming through the lens and adjust the SHUTTER speed and the APERTURE to produce a correctly exposed picture. *See Iris.*

AUTO-FOCUS   Many video and still cameras and camcorders have a useful facility that will automatically FOCUS the LENS on a subject or whatever the camera is pointed at. This generally works well, but occasionally can cause a few problems. If the light is very low, the

Typing script into autocue

auto-focus system may hunt for an image to focus on. If something or someone moves in front of the camera, then it might refocus on the new moving image. If the subject is not centrally located in the frame, the lens may focus on the background, leaving your subject OUT OF FOCUS. If there is something in the FOREGROUND, such as the wire netting of a tennis court, the auto-focus may decide to focus on that rather than the interesting match being played.

AVID Trade name for an industry standard computer-based video EDITING system, both online and offline *(see Online Edit, Offline Edit)*. Avid produces recognised digital standard equipment for professionals from video, **AUDIO** and film to **ANIMATION, SPECIAL EFFECTS** and streaming media. Avid's products are used throughout the world to make broadcast television, commercials, music videos and **CDs**, corporate productions and major motion pictures. These include Avid Film Composer for film-based productions, Avid Xpress and Avid Media Composer offline systems for television production, and Avid News Cutter XP for news. Avid Symphony is a high-end online system. *See **Adobe Premiere, Final Cut Pro**.*

B

BABY LEGS   Colloquial name for a low camera **TRIPOD** with shorter than average legs or supports. It allows the camera to be mounted much closer to the ground than a traditional tripod. Used for taking **LOW-ANGLE SHOTS**, or fitting the camera and tripod into restricted spaces.

BACK ANNO   Colloquial shorthand for back announcement on radio or TV. A comment made by the presenter at the end (back) of a magazine **ITEM, INTERVIEW**, news item or piece of music, which gives brief details of the contributor and the subject, e.g. 'the Prime Minister of Australia on the line from Sydney, commenting on today's Pacific summit'. Can also be a few words by the **CONTINUITY ANNOUNCER** at the end of a programme.

BACKGROUND   Short for background information or research throughout the media. In an article or magazine, the background is that part of the article that contextualises the story and fills the reader in on what led up to the events. Also means a file or files with press cuttings and other relevant information about a particular story, event or celebrity, e.g. 'Have you got the background on Britney Spears?'

BACKGROUND MUSIC   Music that is part of the **SOUNDTRACK** of a film, TV or radio programme. Adds to the emotional or dramatic significance of the story, or enhances the meaning of a scene. Background music is usually specially written or adapted for the soundtrack of a film, and can be released on **CD**. Any commercial CDs used in a media product that is for sale or to be broadcast must have permission from the relevant **COPYRIGHT** holders or their agents. *See Bed, MCPS, PRS.*

BACKING TRACK   Music that provides the instrumental background to the voice of a singer. Typically a pre-recorded music **TRACK** that may include backing vocals that a singer can hear through headphones (in an **AUDIO** studio), a loudspeaker (*see Foldback*) or an earpiece if on stage or appearing in a TV show. The singer has to sing into his or her **MICROPHONE** in tune with the backing track, and make sure he or she comes in at the right point, especially after an instrumental middle eight, as well as harmonising with the music.

BACK LIGHT   Film or TV light placed behind the subject, often mounted high. The amount of light can be controlled with **BARN DOORS**. Used to illuminate the back or side of the subject to create depth and solidity by making the subject stand out from the background. Often used to highlight an actress's hair and create a halo effect. *See Three-Point Lighting.*

BACK PROJECTION   Formerly used in film to create the look of a location by projecting a moving image of the location on to a screen behind the actors, who are in a specially set up

STUDIO. For example, often used in interior car sequences to create the effect of the street receding through the rear window as the car moves along. Common in Hollywood films up to the 1950s; then the introduction of lightweight cameras made it possible and more realistic to film on LOCATION. The technique is now used effectively in digital form. In TV it is called CHROMAKEY or BLUESCREEN. *See Bluescreen, Post-production.*

BACK STORY   They use this word a lot in Hollywood. It relates to a movie SCRIPT. The back story is that part of a character's past life that takes place before the first scene of a movie. This might be the fact that he had a violent father, which affects events on the screen. It is also the events, or the lines of DIALOGUE in a SCREENPLAY that tell the AUDIENCE something extra that happened before the timescale of the movie. It is the events that the scriptwriter knows, and that inform aspects of a film but do not necessarily happen during the film. The back story may show a protagonist's internal desires and the reasons behind the desperate search to fulfil his or her goals. On one level, the back story is evident in the details of a character's upbringing or former marriages, and on a deeper level it can inform the psychological impetus behind a character's actions. *See Flashback, Script, Writing for Television.*

BACK TIMING   Refers to the way a radio or TV programme (or CD/TAPE/MINIDISC) is timed by counting down backwards from the end of the programme. This will show exactly how much time is left before the programme ends. Useful in juggling the length of ITEMS, especially 'live' INTERVIEWS. It allows the PRODUCER/PRESENTER/PRODUCTION team to see at any point how many minutes and seconds are left in the programme, and come out on time. *See Duration.*

BAFFLE   Sound. A screen or moveable panel found in a sound STUDIO. Used to restrict sound from echoing around the studio or to protect a particular MICROPHONE from a sound source. The overall quality of the sound can be adjusted for a particular effect by careful positioning of the baffles.

BAFTA   British Academy of Film and Television Arts, 195 Piccadilly, London W1V 0LN www.bafta.org Promotes best possible practice and creative standards in film and TV production with a regular programme of lectures and workshops for members, including students. Hosts annual BAFTA awards for excellence in a wide range of skill, craft and creative areas of film and TV.

BALANCE   News. Means to ensure that both sides of an argument, or political spectrum, are reflected in a programme. Both content and actual DURATION of each side's contribution within the programme can be taken into account when considering programme balance. Also, programmes offering different points of view may be balanced over a period of time.

Audio. To balance SOUND is to create a pleasing sound mix. When recording music or speech, to achieve the right timbre and the right sound levels of different instruments, the engineer will balance all the microphone outputs, e.g. a vocalist can be heard above the accompanying instruments in a way that resembles a live concert. Balance also describes the choice of microphones and their positions to pick up a good sound signal and to discriminate against background noise or other unwanted sound sources. The aim is to obtain an appropriate blend of direct to indirect sound that gives an AUDIO impression of the occasion, whether it is a concert or a cricket match. *See Audio Mixer, Dub.*

BANDWIDTH   The FREQUENCY range of a transmitting channel. Determines the quality of the signal it carries. Broader bandwidth carries a higher-quality signal. Also refers to the speed of an internet connection measured in kilobits per second (kbps). *See Broadband, Modem.*

BANNER   Print. The main headline that runs across the top of a newspaper page.

BARB   Broadcasters Audience Research Board. The main organisation in the UK for producing TV AUDIENCE statistics, which make up the RATINGS for each TV channel. Other than the information freely available on its website, BARB data is only available to BARB subscribers, for an annual registration fee (currently £3500), together with an annual subscription fee, depending on the nature of the customer's business. BARB figures look like those shown in the table below.

Typical week
Hours of viewing, share of audience and reach: including timeshift

Channel	Average weekly viewing (hrs:mins)*	Share of total viewing %	% Average daily reach	% Weekly reach
ALL/ANY TV	23:04	100.0	74.3	92.2
BBC1 (incl. Breakfast News)	5:59	25.9	53.8	85.4
BBC2	2:32	11.0	35.0	74.1
TOTAL BBC1/BBC2	8:31	36.9	60.3	88.1
ITV (incl. GMTV)	5:39	24.5	49.5	83.1
CHANNEL 4/S4C	2:04	9.0	31.2	70.8
CHANNEL 5	1:31	6.6	20.5	52.4
TOTAL/ANY				
COMM. TERR. TV	9:15	40.1	60.0	88.0
Other viewing	5:19	23.0	28.1	42.4

*per person

© **BARB**

BARN DOORS   Device with hinged metal flaps, usually four, that can be attached to the front of a TV or film lamp. Controls spillage of light into unwanted areas, and restricts the direction and size of the light. Is both pivotal and rotatable so that the light beam can be shaped.

BARS (colour bars)   Vertical strips or bars of colour generated by a video camera or video recorder/player and used to LINE UP the picture. This is to make sure the colours generated by the device are acceptable. Recorded at the beginning of a new tape inserted in a camcorder so that the tape can be lined up correctly on a compatible VCR. *See Line Up.*

Lamp with barn doors

BASS CUT   Audio. A system for cutting or restricting the lowest bass **FREQUENCIES** in a **SOUND** signal. Some **MICROPHONES** have a bass cut switch to turn off some of the lower frequencies to help reduce 'boom' or 'rumble', those unwanted base notes that may make a voice difficult to listen to.

BATCH DIGITISING   Process of recording video **CLIPS** (as data) from a video player or camcorder onto the **HARD DRIVE** of a computer editing system so they can be edited. The video **RUSHES** are viewed and the required clips selected with their **TIME CODES**. These clips can then be loaded onto the editing system, either one by one or in a batch or group. The system takes time to find each clip and **DIGITISE** it. This is speeded up if the clips that have already been selected can be digitised together by utilising the batch option in the software. *See Adobe Premiere, Digital Editing.*

BATTERIES   Several types are used in media production. Most common are alkaline batteries – AA and AAA – which are widely available and used for powering portable sound recorders, microphones and other smaller pieces of kit. Buy best quality. Always have spares. Rechargeable alkaline batteries are available. Typically, these can be recharged up to 50 times. Most video camcorders use NiCad or NiMH.

NiCad, nickel-cadmium, batteries are rechargeable and robust, and relatively inexpensive, but can be heavy, dislike hot conditions and suffer from memory problems. This means they have to be completely run down, or conditioned, before being recharged, or they will not go back to the original fully charged power. If put on to charge before fully depleted they will only charge up to (i.e. remember) the level they were run down to in use. After several rechargings, the battery life will be much shorter unless conditioned each time.

NiMH, nickel-metal hydride, batteries are rechargeable and strong, cost more, but are much less prone to memory problems and can be used more often. Typically, NiMH batteries can be recharged up to 500 times and will self-discharge if left unused. Generally, within 30 to 60 days, batteries will become completely drained. Recharge before using. Good for video cameras. Li-ion, or lithium ion, batteries may cost more, but work extremely well and do not suffer from memory problems. Good in hot and cold weather. Good for digital cameras.

BATTERY BELT A belt with a number of battery cells attached to it. Typically worn by the **CAMERAMAN** as a source of power for the camera. Allows flexibility and movement for cameraman and camera, especially for **HAND HELD** shots.

BCU Big Close-Up. Refers to the size of a person or object in the **FRAME**. A BCU of a person, typically, is a shot of the eyes and mouth, cutting off most of the forehead and most of the chin. A BCU of an object fills the frame with a detail of the design of a Greek vase or a detail of a piece of equipment. *See Shot Size.*

BECTU Broadcasting, Entertainment, Cinematograph and Theatre Union, 111 Wardour Street, London W1V 4AY www.bectu.org.uk The largest union in the media representing technical and craft production staff in broadcasting, film and theatre, and many non-technical staff. Offers a range of useful services to members, including legal representation and tax advice.

BED Music, typically instrumental, used as a background for a presenter to talk over in a radio programme. Some popular music stations use a rhythmic bed under all speech **ITEMS** to give the impression that popular music is being played all the time. Often used in radio commercials and information slots.

BEST BOY The electrician who acts as the assistant to the chief electrician, or **GAFFER**, on a film set or TV drama shoot. *See Sparks.*

BETACAM SP Broadcast quality **VIDEOTAPE** format. Developed by Sony with 12.65mm (0.5 inch) wide, metal-particle tape in a cassette. Standard analogue tape format for news and factual programmes throughout the 1990s and still used throughout the world, but now being overtaken by **DIGITAL** formats such as **DV**.

BETACAM SX A broadcast-quality digital tape **FORMAT**. Developed by Sony using MPEG–2 **COMPRESSION**.

BFI British Film Institute, 21 Stephen Street, London W1P 1PL www.bfi.org.uk Important organisation for promoting and conserving film in the UK. Runs educational courses, has a very good film and visual media library, runs the National Film Theatre in London and publishes a regular magazine, *Sight and Sound.*

BIMA British Interactive Multimedia Association, 5–6 Clipstone Street, London W1P 7EB The trade association for people and organisations working in the MULTIMEDIA industry.

BIT A binary digit. A unit in DIGITAL technology. *See Byte.*

BITC *See Burnt-In Time Code.*

BLEED Print. Printed material – text or pictures – that goes over the edges of the page, sometimes into another page, as in a CENTRESPREAD. A picture that bleeds off the page becomes the page edge and does not leave the normal white margin between the picture and the edge of the page. *See Copy, Double Page Spread.*

BLIMP A soundproof housing that muffles the SOUND of a movie or TV camera's mechanism. Used in quiet LOCATIONS so that camera noise is not picked up by the MICROPHONES. Also the name for a camera housing with other uses, e.g. an UNDERWATER BLIMP, a specially constructed waterproof housing that covers the entire camera so it can be used underwater, usually only to a limited depth.

BLOCKING The planning process where the DIRECTOR goes through the moves and positions suggested for the actors, before filming begins. The term was first used in the theatre. SCENES can be blocked on set or in rehearsal or both. Can include camera positioning and suggestions for setting up lights.

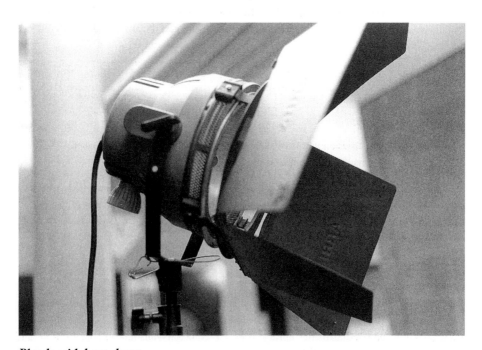

Blonde with barn doors

BLONDE   Powerful, variable-beam film light. A two-KILOWATT (2000-watt) quartz iodine light with a moving REFLECTOR focusing mechanism, so called because it has a yellow (blonde) head or metal casing. Standard portable light used throughout the TV industry. *See Redhead.*

BLOW UP   Print. To enlarge a photograph or section of a photograph.

Film. The enlargement of a FRAME or section of a frame. Refers to the way a smaller FORMAT film is enlarged to a larger format, e.g. 16mm film is blown up to 35mm for theatrical projection in a cinema. *See PBU.*

BLUE GEL   Lighting. Special blue, heat-resistant, plastic sheeting that can be bought in a roll. Used to put over a film lamp to match the COLOUR TEMPERATURE of daylight in a film lighting set-up. *See Gel.*

BLUESCREEN   TV and film. Technique that allows one image to be overlaid on part of another image. The FOREGROUND image, which is usually an actor or PRESENTER, is filmed against a large, carefully lit, blue sheet or screen in a STUDIO or on LOCATION. Film can use a green screen – it does the same job. The screen can include a blue/green floor and walls to provide the entire background to the shot. This blue or green background is then replaced (or KEYED) in POST-PRODUCTION with another image to create a matched composite picture. With this technique, actors can be keyed into futuristic sets or surf on giant virtual waves, without leaving the studio. Computer-generated imagery (CGI) can also be used, as in the *Star Wars* films. Also known in TV as CHROMAKEY. Using bluescreen is useful in doing INTERVIEWS. The interview is videoed against a blue curtain or a portable blue background. In post-production the blue background is replaced by moving pictures of the DIRECTOR'S choice. These pictures are often relevant to the subject of the interview and give it an extra dimension. With bluescreen, you do not have to send your REPORTER to Los Angeles to do a story on the Oscars. You can put him or her in a small studio specially designed for the purpose, with blue floor and walls. Modern sophisticated bluescreen studios allow the director to cut between CLOSE-UPS and LONG SHOTS. Carefully selected pictures of Los Angeles will replace the blue and the reporter will appear to be there, in the heart of the city, even seeming to walk around and sit down on a bench in Universal Studios. *See Post-Production.*

BLUETOOTH   New communications technology yet to take off in a big way. Bluetooth is short-range wireless connection between telephones, computers, PRINTERS and other devices such as a video cameras. Smart mobile phones use bluetooth technology to form a wireless link with a docking station in a car, so that the mobile does not need to be plugged in.

BNC   Professional type of connector, or plug, for video cables that has a twist lock to form a safe, strong connection. *See Jack Plug.*

BODY TEXT   Print. The main part of the text of an article in a newspaper or MAGAZINE that comes after the subheading and opening paragraph.

BOLD   Print. **Text that is printed darker, like this, to stand out.** Also does the same job on computer word-processing software.

BOOM Moveable arm to hold a MICROPHONE or camera. In a TV STUDIO, refers to a sound boom – a mobile piece of sound equipment used in large TV studios. A microphone is mounted in a cradle on a telescopic tube, which is fixed to an adjustable column on a specially designed three-wheeled trolley. The microphone is swung out over the top of cameras to keep out of SHOT and get the microphone as near as possible to the CONTRIBUTOR, for optimum sound quality. A skilled operator sits on a seat on the boom trolley and controls the reach, direction and angle of the microphone with a system of wire pulleys. This allows the microphone to follow the action and pick up a natural sound perspective. *See Fish Pole.*

BOUNCE LIGHT A SOFT LIGHT source produced by pointing a film light at a white reflective surface such as a REFLECTOR, so that the light bounces off the surface. Can be used to light a domestic room by using a BLONDE film lamp to bounce light off a white ceiling.

BOX WIPE An electronically created visual effect produced by a VISION MIXING DESK in a TV STUDIO control GALLERY. Looks like a very small rectangular box within the centre of the FRAME that contains the new picture. As the rectangle grows larger, so the new picture wipes out the previous one. *See DVE.*

BPI British Phonographic Industry www.bpi.co.uk The BPI represents the interests of over 200 British record companies, accounting for 90 per cent of recorded music output in the UK. *See IFPI.*

BRACE A strut used to hold up a FLAT or other part of the set in a TV STUDIO, film set or in the theatre. A typical strut is about two metres long and has a hook at each end. One end hooks onto a special fitting on the flat, and the other hooks into a weighted base unit.

BRITISH FILM INSTITUTE *See BFI.*

BRITISH UNIVERSITIES FILM & VIDEO COUNCIL 77 Wells Street, London W1P 3RE www.bufvc.ac.uk Represents institutions of higher education in the UK. Aims to promote the PRODUCTION, study and use of film, television and related media in higher education. Publishes a magazine, *Viewfinder,* three times a year for members. Funded by grant and subscriptions.

BROADBAND Refers to a fast internet connection with permanent access. To send good-quality VIDEO and MULTIMEDIA material through the internet reliably you need a connection that is faster than the average 56kbps (*see Bandwidth*) home MODEM. Known as broadband, this includes ADSL, and cable and satellite connections, which are up to ten times the speed of an ordinary modem, and have always-on functionality, for a monthly subscription. Commercially, broadband offers considerable possibilities, such as video on demand. In the US, broadband is well advanced. Subscribers are offered a huge choice of films and TV programmes from the ARCHIVES of the major studios, including Universal Pictures, Warner, Dreamworks SKG, MGM and Walt Disney. These can be streamed over the net to their PC for a monthly subscription. Feature films are purchased on a pay-per-view basis. Broadband also allows teleconferencing and interactive multimedia functions. Definitely the future for internet connections. Several websites are involved with broadband.

www.broadband.blueyonder.co.uk is a dedicated broadband **PORTAL**. It offers film previews, music video **CLIPS** and chat rooms, as well as games. For news fans, www.itv.com offers a gateway to over 300 TV stations around the world. For movie lovers www.ifilm.com offers a vast archive of on-demand international independent movies. For **ANIMATION** and multimedia, try www.shockwave.com.

BROADCASTING STANDARDS Regulations and guidelines under which broadcasters work in the UK, Europe and in the US. In the UK, the BBC issues guidelines for production teams, and the governors of the BBC are required by the government to maintain high standards in public service broadcasting. The **INDEPENDENT TELEVISION COMMISSION** (ITC) regulates ITV and other broadcasters in the UK, including advertisers.

BROADSHEET A large A1 size daily newspaper, such as the *Guardian*, or Sunday paper, such as *The Sunday Times*. Prints more **NEWS** and covers more serious issues, such as world news and international current affairs, than a **TABLOID**. Tends to have a daily circulation of around half a million. Relies on quality advertising for revenue.

BROWSER Multimedia. Software that links a user's computer with the internet. Opens up websites and offers a search facility, e.g. Internet Explorer or Netscape Navigator.

BRUTE A large carbon arc film lamp, typically of 22.5 **KILOWATTS**. Can be **FOCUSED**. Used on large film productions as a major light source. The arc lamp was the earliest source of light used in filmmaking.

BUDGET The total amount of money agreed for making a film, TV or radio programme. Low budget means less than the average and high budget means more. In TV and radio, it is considered to be very unprofessional to spend more than the agreed amount and go over budget, although some filmmakers can make a virtue of it (James Cameron with *Titanic*). Under budget means bringing in the production for less than the agreed budget. A typical TV programme budget is made up of many elements:

- **RESOURCES – VIDEOTAPE**, lights, camera and **SOUND** equipment;
- people and their time – film **CREW** and production staff;
- subsistence – food, travel and accommodation;
- insurance – public liability insurance, kit insurance;
- office and communications – computer, fax, phone and mobile;
- **TALENT – PRESENTERS** and/or actors;
- **PROPS**, costume and make-up;
- **COPYRIGHT** and programme rights;
- any special equipment;
- **POST-PRODUCTION** – can be very costly if there are any **SPECIAL EFFECTS**.

Radio budgets are much less than those for a similar-length TV programme. A **PRODUCER/REPORTER** can do much of the **LOCATION** recording with just a **MINIDISC** recorder. Radio drama is almost always produced in the studio, but well-known actors and SCRIPT adaptation can be expensive.

BULK ERASER   Electrical equipment that 'wipes' or demagnetises magnetic AUDIO or VIDEOTAPE. Useful for recycling tapes, but keep your wristwatch well away from it.

BULLETIN   NEWS bulletin. A summary of up-to-date news delivered by a newsreader or PRESENTER on radio or TV. The news presenter on TV reads from AUTOCUE in a STUDIO with remote-controlled cameras. Some channels use a VIRTUAL STUDIO.

BURNT-IN TIME CODE   Video. Also known as BITC. A method of showing in vision on PLAYBACK the TIME CODE (TC) recorded onto a VIDEOTAPE during the recording process. An electronic reader reads the time code and transfers it onto the pictures as white numbers on a black background. Pictures with TC are then recorded onto another tape. The process is known as burning in. BITC is usually in the lower third of the screen.

BUZZ TRACK   *See Atmos.*

B/W   Abbreviation of black and white. Refers to both non-colour FILM STOCK and a colour television picture that has been altered to black and white only.

BYLINE   Print. The name of the writer of an ARTICLE in a publication, usually placed under the title or at the end of the piece.

BYTE   Unit of DIGITAL technology. Measurement for data storage is by the number of bytes. One byte equals eight bits. One thousand bytes is called a KILOBYTE (KB); 1,048,576 bytes is known as a MEGABYTE (Mb); a GIGABYTE (Gb) is 1024 megabytes. Modern AUDIO, photographic and video recording systems are digital. Still and video pictures require a lot of space, or gigabytes, to store the digital data. *See Compression, Format.*

CACHE Multimedia. That part of the computer memory that is set aside for the temporary storage of data. A decent-sized cache, e.g. 512K, can speed up the way the computer processes data. Contains information such as directions to files that are accessed frequently. *See Kilobyte, Compression.*

CALL SHEET Paperwork used in broadcasting and film. Issued to cast and CREW before a shoot or radio outside broadcast (OB), detailing where everyone has to be and when. Can be a short document with production contact details, date, times and exact LOCATIONS for a one- or two-day shoot, or a more complex multi-page affair. Created by the DIRECTOR/ PRODUCER or the production assistant (PA) for a factual programme, and by the production manager's office for a drama. Typical call sheet for a shoot such as ITV's *The Bill* would include detailed arrangements for picking up actors, arrival on set, time in make-up, time to fit/collect costumes and times on set, as well as meal times and the WRAP. There will be a full list of all crew contact details and other important information, such as the power source for each location (*see Genny*), contact names for the police, local hospital and parking arrangements, as well as the all-important rendezvous (*see RV*) points. A call sheet for a TV production can look like this:

Programme Title: CLUB CITY
CALL SHEET
THURSDAY 2 OCTOBER 2003

Pogo Productions

Director: John Greeves	Mobile	Home tel. no.
Producer: Tina Eastwoode		
Presenter: Sally Friedan		
Camera: Graham Cranston		
Sound: Julian Harknell		

CALL TIME	0900
RV	West Pier Entrance
	Brighton, Sussex
PARKING	Parking in Regency Car Park (get receipt)
	Crew car has special permission to park temporarily on the Lower Promenade.

LUNCH	1300–1400 The Beach Club and bar
BREAK	1600–2100
LATE FILMING	2100–0200

OVERNIGHT ACCOMMODATION Brunswick Square Hotel, Brunswick Square.
Parking arranged. Tel: 0101010

STOCK	DVCAM tapes supplied by cameraman
KIT	Camera: Sony DSR–500 wsp Widescreen 16:9 format
	Lights: 4 × 800W redhead kit. Single blonde 1 × 2000W
	Radio mics
TIME CODE	Start at roll 29
SHOOTING	Further filming in a 5 × 25 min. series about the club scene throughout Britain. AM exteriors and interviews on the beach. PM exteriors, Brighton, and interviews. Evening: nightclub interior and exterior shots, interviews. Sound: recordings and tracks from club sound system, and special locked-off interior lighting effects.

CAMERA   Portable equipment that enables moving and still images to be recorded onto VIDEOTAPE, disc or celluloid film. All cameras share features such as a LENS, SHUTTER and IRIS or APERTURE control. What has changed is the way the image is recorded. Feature films are still shot on film, by a film camera. Television relies more and more on DIGITAL video camcorders for acquisition of material. There are many different recording FORMATS to store the data acquired by the camera. At the top end is DIGITAL BETACAM, developed by Sony. A modern camcorder such as a Sony DVW–790 wsp, can be hired for about £250 per day; using 12-bit signal processing it is able to record digitally up to forty minutes per tape with very high-QUALITY pictures and SOUND. At the lower end, but still of broadcastable standard is a professional camcorder, such as a Sony DSR–PD250 3CCD camera, which can be hired for about £100 per day. This can record for up to sixty minutes on DV, and has an optional ANAMORPHIC lens for shooting in WIDESCREEN format. In the US and Japan, high definition TV (HDTV) is gaining acceptance because of its superior near-film quality. HDTV domestic TV sets are needed to view the format and these are still expensive. The standard for feature films is 35mm. Widescreen formats up to 70mm film are also used. Some of the film distribution companies are seeking to use very high quality digital cameras to make films that can be projected digitally in cinemas and distributed from a central source. The cinema would pick up the encoded signal from a satellite dish, thus cutting down the costs of transporting, distributing and projecting large reels of 35mm film.

CAMERA CARD   List of SHOTS, camera moves and other essential information, made up on a card and customised for every camera in a multi-camera studio or LOCATION shoot. Created initially by the production team, but adapted by each CAMERA OPERATOR to make sure he or she can achieve each shot. *See OB, TV Studio.*

CAMERA CRANE   Flexible hydraulic arm that can rise, like a crane, high above the set. Has

16mm Arriflex film camera

Camera crane with camera operator and director in India

vertical and sideways movement with a camera mounting at the end. A film camera crane may carry the CAMERA, CAMERA OPERATOR and the DIRECTOR.

CAMERA LEFT   Refers to the direction in which the subject is looking – in this case to the left – from the point of view of the camera. A subject looking camera left is looking towards the left-hand side of the FRAME, as the image is seen on the screen by the camera and, therefore, the viewer. This is a mirror image of what the subject is actually doing. From the subject's point of view, he or she is looking towards his or her right. *See Camera Right.*

CAMERAMAN/CAMERAWOMAN   Term used to describe the male or female chief operator of a moving-image camera, especially on a one-camera programme shoot. Knowledge and understanding of how the camera works is necessary, as well as an intuitive, artistic and creative eye for framing a SCENE. You also need stamina to work long hours, and good social skills as there are a lot of people to meet and get on with, especially if you are FREELANCE. The cameraman or camerawoman will be carefully briefed by the DIRECTOR about what the programme is about and, particularly, what is required from the day's shoot. He or she will set up the lighting, FRAME the SHOTS and work closely with the director, suggesting additional ways of shooting a scene. A modern TV cameraman/woman, working on a variety of LOCATIONs will do everything – position and set up the lights, operate the camera and maybe

Camera operator

even set up the **SOUND**. With modern lightweight **DV** cameras, factual programmes can be shot by a director/cameraman/camerawoman, who can also set up the sound for a straightforward **INTERVIEW**. On a larger-scale drama or movie there will be a **CAMERA OPERATOR** and a **LIGHTING CAMERAMAN** also known as the **CINEMATOGRAPHER**.

CAMERA OPERATOR   The member of a TV or film **CREW** who physically operates the camera and **FRAMES** the **SHOTS**. Could work on an **OB** as part of a team, operating a video camera covering a football match or similar event, or on a drama, operating a 35mm camera depending on skills, experience and preference. For smaller productions or factual programmes, the camera operator also directs how the lighting should be set up. For a movie, the camera operator will work to the **LIGHTING CAMERAMAN** or **CINEMATOGRAPHER**.

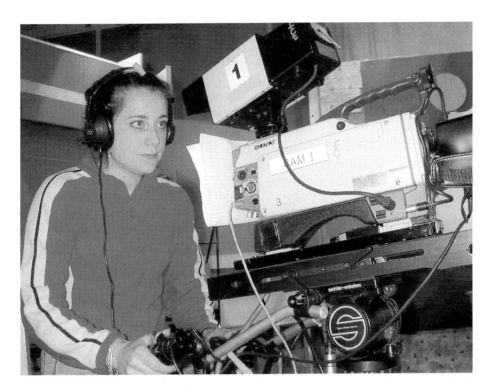

TV studio camera operator

CAMERA RIGHT   Refers to the direction in which the subject is looking – in this case to the right – from the point of view of the camera and the viewer. A subject looking camera right is looking towards the right-hand side of the **FRAME** when the image is seen on the screen. From the subject's point of view, he or she is looking towards his or her left. *See Camera Left.*

CAMERA SCRIPT A SCRIPT for a LIVE or recorded TV show that contains all the programme material and how it is to be recorded in the TV STUDIO. The SHOT numbers, camera numbers and positions are marked alongside the full script. Relevant technical directions are included. Created by the DIRECTOR and the PA for use in a TV studio GALLERY. Distributed to all members of the production team, including set DESIGNER, costume, make-up and SOUND. Heavily used by the FLOOR MANAGER to get everything in place for the show.

CAN Round metal tin that can hold one or more reels of film, depending on size. This is where the expression 'in the can' comes from. It means that a SCENE has been SHOT or recorded on VIDEOTAPE and is safely stored away, ready to be EDITED. If a whole film is in the can, it has been completed and is ready for distribution.

CANS Colloquial for headphones – expression used particularly in radio.

CAPTION Print. The words underneath a printed picture or photograph that describe it and/or name the people in it. The text that accompanies and relates to artwork or a photograph in a print publication.

TV and film. Any text or GRAPHIC design inserted or SUPERIMPOSED in a TV programme or film. In its most basic form, a caption is white lettering, or a picture, pasted onto black card and put in front of a camera. Captions are now created DIGITALLY with dedicated caption-generating equipment, such as ASTON. A GRAPHICS DESIGNER can create moving-image graphics on high-end equipment made by a specialist company like QUANTEL, and then put the images onto VIDEOTAPE for inclusion in the programme. *See Name Super, CGI.*

CARDIOID Audio. MICROPHONE with a heart-shaped pick-up pattern around the top of the MIC. Particularly useful for doing an INTERVIEW with one other person. Held between interviewer and INTERVIEWEE, it provides a good SOUND image without picking up too much extraneous noise. Good all-round mic, useful in many radio situations. *See Hyper Cardioid.*

CASSETTE Plastic casing for AUDIO or VIDEOTAPE. Audio cassettes are now an almost obsolete form of recording and playing back music, e.g. from a portable cassette player such as a Walkman. Videotapes and DAT tapes come in cassette form to protect the tape and for ease of use. *See Format.*

CASTING The process of finding, AUDITIONING and selecting the right actors/TALENT for a particular radio, TV or film production. A CASTING AGENT may be employed to help find suitable actors to audition. *See Presenter.*

CASTING AGENT Professional person or team with encyclopaedic knowledge of a large number of actors, especially newcomers and unusual performers. Employed by film companies and TV drama productions to find actors to fill particular roles. A casting agent will trawl theatres, drama schools and fringe productions up and down the country, looking for new TALENT to offer film PRODUCERS and TV DIRECTORS.

CASTING OFF   Print. Estimating the final length of a newspaper ARTICLE by taking into account the number of words and the size of the TYPEFACE.

CATHODE RAY TUBE   The glass picture tube that houses the electron gun and phosphor-coated face-plate that create images on a conventional TV set. A standard single tube creates all three video colours, red, green and blue (RGB), at the face-plate. Projection televisions have a high-output cathode ray tube for each colour, which projects a converged, full-colour image onto the screen.

CCD   Charge-Coupled Diode. A supersensitive light sensor that reacts to light in a DIGITAL camcorder or video camera in a similar manner to the way film reacts to light in a film camera. One or more of these sensors picks up light from the images the LENS sees and converts it into electrical signals, which can be processed and stored on VIDEOTAPE. The best cameras have a three-chip CCD, one chip for each of the primary colours that video uses: red, green and blue. Each chip collects upwards of 300,000 bits of information. *See Compression, Format, Pixel, RGB.*

CD   Compact Disc. DIGITAL sound recording on a shiny 12cm plastic disc that is played back by laser beam technology. Superseded the 12-inch vinyl long-playing record as the preferred method of listening to recorded music. Recordable CDs are used to store digital data on a computer via suitable CD-writing software. *See CD-R, CD-RW, CD-ROM.*

CD-R   Compact Disc-Recordable. CD that can record up to 700 MEGABYTES of data from a computer using the appropriate software and recordable disc drive.

CD-ROM   Compact Disc-Read Only Memory. FORMAT for storing DIGITAL data, such as computer files or digital pictures, artwork etc. Stores about 450 times more data than a FLOPPY DISK. *See CD.*

CD-RW   Compact Disc-Rewritable. CD disc FORMAT that allows repeated recording of data onto the disc.

CELEBRITIES   People who have acquired celebrity status, and are, therefore, 'desirable' guests on a TV or radio programme, include actors, pop stars, musicians, sports people and people 'created by TV' such as PRESENTERS. The jury is still out for serving politicians, but some former politicians definitely have celebrity status, e.g. Bill Clinton or Jeffrey Archer. Notoriety does not seem to be a barrier to becoming a celeb. The dividing line between celebrity and ordinary CONTRIBUTOR may sometimes be difficult to define; if in doubt, treat as celebrity.

CENTRESPREAD   Print. Feature ARTICLE that runs over the two centre facing pages of a publication. These pages are effectively one page folded in half, so the pages can BLEED over into each other for an effective display. *See Copy, Double Page Spread.*

CFU (Children's Film Unit)   Email: cfilmunit@aol.com website: www.btinternet.com/ ~cfu Registered educational charity formed in 1981. Unique film production unit for children under 16. Aim is to actively involve children who are interested in film work, and provide opportunities for them to learn all aspects of filmmaking and take part in making feature films. Very hands on. Holds regular workshops in the holidays and after school. At least one film is made by the unit each year, under the guidance of professional tutors. Children are involved at every level, from SCRIPT to POST-PRODUCTION. They are trained to operate CAMERA and SOUND equipment, set the lighting and do CONTINUITY, as well as act.

CGA   Computer-Generated Animation. This is the name for the sophisticated and complex world of computer animation in films such as *Shrek*, as well as the computer-generated extraordinary effects in *Spider-Man*. As computers have become more powerful and can store many GIGABYTES of data, so it has become possible to build layers of computer-generated images and add them to LIVE ACTION. One of the first major feature films to use CGA effectively to represent people was *Titanic*.

CGI   Computer-Generated Imaging. Digital technology that allows sophisticated, three-dimensional-looking and often naturalistic pictures to be created on a computer. These images may be integrated into a movie or TV programme to create a particular effect, e.g. the changing seasons sequence in the film *Notting Hill*. **See CGA**.

CHANGING BAG   Film. A black cloth bag used on LOCATION by the ASSISTANT CAMERAMAN to load and unload a film MAGAZINE. Specially designed with tight-fitting armholes so that the roll of film can be loaded by feel into the magazine or unloaded into a film CAN, without exposing it to light. Needs experience and manual dexterity to load the film properly.

CHAPERONE   Experienced adult who looks after a child actor or under-16 CONTRIBUTOR to a film or TV show.

CHEQUERBOARD   Refers to a method of EDITING, both on film and video, that uses two rolls of pictures as an A roll and a B roll. Where a TRANSITION from one sequence of images to another is required, the first part of the transition is on the A roll and the second part on the B roll. This allows for overlaps between each roll, giving smooth transitions of any length and time. Particularly important for film editing and the NEG CUTTING process.

CHERRY PICKER   Steady, moveable platform that can hold a camera and CAMERA OPERATOR. Can be raised or lowered hydraulically in order to take an OVERHEAD SHOT or HIGH-ANGLE SHOT. Usually mounted on a vehicle for manoeuvrability.

CHILDREN (in productions)   Children under 16 may be employed in TV, film or radio productions. There are strict rules about using child actors and CONTRIBUTORS. A licence has to be obtained from the local education authority for all child performances that take place during school hours. A tutor must be provided if the child is on LOCATION or working in the theatre for more than a stipulated number of hours in a week. In a TV studio or on a film set, a CHAPERONE must be provided at all times.

CHILDREN'S FILM UNIT   *See CFU*.

CHROMAKEY   System of overlaying one picture electronically on sections of another picture. Chromakey can be quite simple or fiendishly complicated. At a basic level, a TV

PRESENTER sits in a **TV STUDIO** with a carefully lit blue background behind him or her – known as a **BLUESCREEN**. The blue area that shows up in the picture on the **MONITOR** can be replaced with suitable moving images from a different source, such as pictures of a holiday destination. The blue colour (chroma) is used to **KEY** the other images. For action sequences, where aliens might be attacking a group of actors, say, a whole studio space, including floor and all walls, will be painted blue and carefully lit to avoid shadows. All the blue areas can be replaced with animated (*see CGA*) or **LIVE ACTION** images using chromakey. Using high-end computer power, this is a valuable and extremely flexible technique that can create astonishing visual displays, transporting an actor to the landscape of the moon or making him walk on water. The same technique is used in film, notably in the *Star Wars* films. Sometimes, in film production, a **GREEN SCREEN** is used. *See Virtual Studio*.

CINEMATOGRAPHER The most important person on a movie set apart from the **DIRECTOR**. Responsible for the overall look of a film, working closely with the **DIRECTOR**. In overall charge of the lighting crew and the **CAMERA OPERATORS**. Liaises with the **GAFFER** as to what lights to use and where to place them. Selects **LENSES** and **FILTERS** for the camera, as well as framing the **SHOT** and setting up camera moves and angles. Some movie directors, such as Sam Mendes, give great credit to the cinematographer on their films, e.g. the Oscar-winning films *Road to Perdition* and *American Beauty*.

CLAPPERBOARD Traditionally, a board in two hinged parts, used to create a loud sharp **SOUND** by bringing the two parts of the board together in a brisk clap. The board has information about the production on it. The visual image of the two parts of the board coming

Clapperboard

together allows the **FILM EDITOR** to synchronise sound and picture (*see Sync*) so that characters will not appear **OUT OF SYNC**. The top part is smaller and is clapped onto the lower larger part on which is marked the **SCENE** number and the **TAKE** number. The date, name of the film or production and the **DIRECTOR** are also usually written on the board for easy recognition and identification. Film productions can now use an electronic clapperboard to give the data in electronic form and a pulse to 'sync up' the film. Recording on **VIDEOTAPE** includes **TIME CODE** so it is no longer necessary to use a clapperboard to sync up each take.

CLIP   Film, video. Describes a small section of **VIDEOTAPE** or film taken from a longer complete film or programme.

CLIPPINGS   Collated **ARTICLES** from newspapers and **MAGAZINES**, filed under name of subject and held in a broadcaster's or newspaper's library. Clippings are called up to use as background information before a **CELEBRITY** or well-known person is interviewed for a publication or a TV or radio programme. Video or **AUDIO** material on a celebrity is held in an **ARCHIVE**, but sometimes it is possible to get **TRANSCRIPTS** of broadcast **INTERVIEWS**.

Close-Up (CU)

CLOCK   TV. Refers to a specially recorded clock-style tape – or digital clock readout – used at the beginning of a **VIDEOTAPED** TV production to show the 30-second (or longer) countdown to the beginning of the actual programme. Includes a special section for the last ten seconds to facilitate a smooth transition into the transmission stream.

CLOSE-UP (CU)   Refers to the size of the image of a person or object in a film or TV **FRAME**. A CU of a person is a shot of the head, with the bottom of the frame just below the chin. An object that fills the frame on its own is also a close-up. *See CU.*

COLLAGE   A collection of different words and pictures taken from print sources and glued onto a page to create an overall effect (from the French word to stick or glue – *coller*); can also be created on a computer. The collage can be scanned into a publishing software package or photographed as a magazine page.

COLOUR BARS   Video test signal in the form of vertical columns of colour from white through yellow, cyan, green, magenta, red, blue and black. Professional camcorders can generate a burst of bars at the beginning of a **VIDEOTAPE** recording. This allows the colour **BALANCE** of the tape to be set up accurately on replay from the colour bars at the front.

COLOURIST   Skilled person who works in **POST-PRODUCTION** to electronically match the colours of all the pictures in a film or TV programme. A programme may contain pictures from many different sources, with a variety of differing colour standards. Even pictures from two rolls of the same type of film may need subtly balancing to match the colours. A colourist can also alter colours to create astounding dramatic effects for a film, video or promo.

COLOUR TEMPERATURE   Lighting. A method of measuring the colour value of a light source. Measured in degrees **KELVIN**. Daylight has a colour temperature of nominally 5500K (Kelvin).

COLUMN   Print. A vertical section that is taller than it is wide in a newspaper containing **COPY**. Colloquial term to describe a regular **ARTICLE** by a journalist in a newspaper, e.g. Libby Purves's column in *The Times*.

COMMAG   Film. Refers to combined magnetic sound. A system on film where the **SOUNDTRACK** is recorded onto the **FILM STOCK** as a magnetic track. It can be projected with a Commag projector.

COMMENTARY   TV and film. Written **SCRIPT** that is recorded by an out-of-vision voice and used to explain or add extra information to relevant pictures. Typically used in **DOCUMENTARY** or factual programmes. A good commentary will be written to work with the way the pictures have been edited. It will not state the obvious or describe anything that can be seen **ON SCREEN**. It will be written in short sentences in a clear, uncluttered style and, generally, in the present tense. Statistical data needs to be written in such a way that it can be easily assimilated by the audience, using phrases like 'one commuter in five' rather than 20 per cent. The person doing the commentary, although an unseen voice, may be the **REPORTER** or

PRESENTER of the programme. Programme-makers like to invite well-known people, who have an interest or relevance to the subject, to do the commentary for their programmes, e.g. David Attenborough might do the commentary on a programme about wildlife in the Arctic. Somewhat confusingly, commentary is not read by a **COMMENTATOR**, who does a different job and will normally work on **LIVE** programmes.

COMMENTATOR   Sound. Person who describes for a media **AUDIENCE** an event or spectacle. It could be an event in the Olympic games or a football match. A commentator for radio will concentrate on describing what is going on and add some analysis. The commentator for a televised event is essentially adding extra information and expert interpretation of the situation rather than describing for the viewer what can be seen on the screen. *See Lip Mic.*

COMMERCIAL RECORDINGS   Refers to recordings of music or speech issued commercially by a record company or publisher. Subject to copyright rules and regulations, a commercial recording can be broadcast or used in a commercial TV or radio programme with the appropriate permissions, payments and licences. Broadcasters have blanket agreements with the larger record companies for using many commercial recordings, but you still need to clear – that is, check with the **COPYRIGHT** holders that permission will be granted to use the recording for your particular production and what the fee will be. *See Production Music, PRS, MCPS, Music Copyright, Play List.*

COMMISSION   Verb – a broadcaster may commission (pay for) a film or TV programme from an independent **PRODUCER**, which means the programme has been agreed with a certain **BUDGET** and can now go ahead (similar to a **CONTRACT**).

Noun – an individual producer may receive a commission (contract) to make a TV or radio programme for a broadcaster. This may or may not include the cost of making the programme. A TV programme may be fully commissioned. The broadcaster pays for all of it and owns the whole programme after it is made. The producer will be paid for the work he or she does on it. *See Commissioning Editor.*

COMMISSIONING EDITOR   Creative executive employed by a broadcaster to sift, select and make decisions on what programmes are to be produced for a particular channel. Broadcasters have a commissioning editor for a genre such as children's, sport, prime time drama, factual or daytime. The commissioning editor's job is to select from hundreds of proposals received each year and choose programmes within the overall **BUDGET** that are suitable for the genre and channel. *See Commission.*

A print publisher will employ a commissioning editor to commission an author or journalist to write a book or magazine article for the publishing house or a particular publication. The job typically involves working with the author on choice of subject, content, style, and use of illustrations as well as seeing the work through to final publication.

CompactFlash   Multimedia. Trade name for a portable memory system used in **DIGITAL CAMERAS** to store images. A good-quality standard 6 × 4-inch picture with high **RESOLUTION** needs about half a **MEGABYTE** of memory with this system. A card with 64 megabytes of memory can store about 120 images, depending on the **QUALITY**.

COMPETITIONS   On-air competitions with prizes are subject to certain restraints and protocols, depending on the broadcasting organisation. Public service broadcasters, such as the BBC, have strict guidelines to stop commercial organisations promoting their products by offering programme-makers free gifts to be used as prizes.

COMPLAINTS   In media, refers to complaints made by the public to broadcast media organisations or their regulatory bodies. A complaint that is upheld by a regulatory body against a broadcaster may require an on-air apology and the broadcaster could be fined.

COMPRESSION   Video. System of reducing or compressing digital data for **TRANSMISSION** or storage. Works by selecting and filtering out some of the less useful information in a **DIGITAL** signal. Visual images require an enormous amount of storage space that would exceed the space available on a manageable system like a **VIDEOTAPE**, CD or **DVD**. To manage this amount of data and to record these images and **SOUND** onto tape, disc or **HARD DISK**, several systems of compression have evolved. Compression works by **SAMPLING** the pictures and sound in a particular digital process. This can be very complex, depending on the **QUALITY** required for the final product. Several compression systems are used in television transmission and production. Many editing systems use **JPEG** compression. MPEG-2 provides much higher compression ratios and is used in transmission systems and DVD. Digital recording systems, such as cameras, also use compression schemes to reduce the amount of data so that it can be stored on small tapes. Sony systems, such as **DIGITAL BETACAM**, **DV** or SX, have different compression ratios. The compression ratio is an expression of how the material is stored. DV has a compression ratio of 5:1. Broadly speaking, approximately five moving-image **FRAMES** are compressed into one. This works by **SAMPLING** each frame and not saving any parts of the frame that do not change, e.g. when a TV journalist records a report from a battle zone, the **SHOT** may have the journalist standing in front of, but some way from, blackened and demolished buildings. The background of the frame may change very little during the course of the report. The compression system will save storage space by only saving the small areas that change in the shot – in this case, the journalist moving. When the tape is replayed, a decoder will 'fill in' the unrecorded areas with reference to a previous complete frame.

COMPRESSION RATIO   *See Compression.*

CONFORM   Video editing. The creation of the master tape from the original source tapes – the **RUSHES**. Conforming for a high-quality video product is done in an **ONLINE** suite. All the editing decisions have been made in the **OFFLINE** editing process and are contained in an **EDL**. These instructions on the EDL can directly control the conforming process. With desktop computer editing something similar to the conforming process is known as **RENDERING**.

CONTINUITY   The process of ensuring that all on-screen material in a **SCENE** relates perfectly in detail and design to all the other scenes in a film or TV drama. Has come to refer to the member of the production team who carries out the task of ensuring continuity, by checking on set, **PROPS**, costume, make-up and position of actors' hands, hair and carried objects (props). Using **DIGITAL** or Polaroid pictures taken at each set-up, the continuity person can check to make sure all details match when the scene is shot again or when the succeeding scene is set up.

CONTINUITY ANNOUNCER The continuity announcer is the off-screen voice that introduces the next programme on broadcast TV or radio. Works with the **TRANSMISSION** suite to make sure the radio station or TV channel runs seamlessly. Is available if there is a technical breakdown of any sort or, very occasionally, will make an announcement if there is a national emergency or a serious newsflash. *See **Commentator**.*

CONTRACTS An agreement between a person offering work or services and an employer. A short- or long-term contract is the main basis for paying personnel working in film, TV and radio. Production, crew and talent will usually have different contracts with different conditions. *See **Contributor's Agreement, Release Form.***

CONTRIBUTOR A person who is selected to take part in a radio or TV programme. May be a paid or non-paid contributor.

CONTRIBUTOR'S AGREEMENT This is a permission form, similar to a **RELEASE FORM**, for someone taking part in a professional media production. This agreement is for a contributor who is making a fairly major contribution to the production, and who will be paid, but who is not covered by any union agreement such as **EQUITY**, the actors' union. This could be an expert or someone who is giving their knowledge and time. *See **Contract**.*

CONTROL ROOM Part of a radio **STUDIO** or music recording complex. The **PRODUCER** and **SOUND** engineer sit at the **SOUND MIXING DESK** in the control room, and can **MONITOR** the sound **OUTPUT** of the studio, either **ON AIR** or for a recording. They have two-way contact with the artist or contributor in the studio. *See **Cue Light**.*

CONVERGENCE Multimedia. Convergence of multimedia technologies allows any **DIGITAL** data to be transmitted by any suitable digital medium. Convergence is the coming together of digital communications, computer-generated graphics, video and **AUDIO**, leading to **INTERACTIVE** media. Linked to a **BROADBAND** telephone system, a domestic TV set becomes a two-way communication module. This provides interactive TV and video games, **EMAIL**, internet access and many other features, as well as a large number of digital TV channels, **PAY PER VIEW** films and digital radio stations.

COOKIE Multimedia. A special type of file, delivered to a computer from a website (usually commercial) to store information about that website on the user's computer **HARD DISK**. Speeds up access to the site next time it is visited.

COOL EDIT PRO Radio. Professional proprietary computer software for digital **NON-LINEAR** sound **EDITING**. Used extensively in commercial radio and by **FREELANCE REPORTERS** and **PRODUCERS**.

COPY Print. The written text of an **ARTICLE** for a print publication.

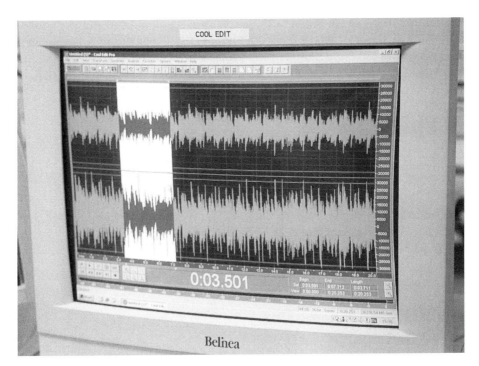

How the screen looks when editing on Cool Edit Pro

COPY-EDITING Print. Checking an **ARTICLE** or any print material for factual accuracy and for any errors in spelling, grammar or **LAYOUT**. Much more than just running it through the spellchecker on the computer.

COPYRIGHT An intellectual property right. It is a way of protecting the tangible result of creative work, such as recorded music or a **SCRIPT**, from being pirated and exploited by someone else. This is not the same as an idea that has not been written down or published, but remains in your head, which is not protected by copyright until it is expressed in a way that can be protected, such as getting it published or registered. Writer Jonathan Swift was instrumental in getting the first Copyright Act established in 1709, through which published books were protected for 21 years. In the twenty-first century, literary, artistic, musical and dramatic works are protected for 70 years. In the UK, the main areas of copyright are covered in the 1988 Copyright, Designs and Patents Act, which seeks to protect the tangible result of creative work from unfair exploitation. Throughout the world, the broad principles of copyright protection remain similar, but the law does vary, between the US and Europe, for example, although more and more steps are being taken to remove such differences. The 1988 Act covers several main areas. The ones that most affect people working in the media are original literary, dramatic, artistic and musical works, including films and broadcast programmes. This is not just film and TV scripts, but magazines, books, stage plays and other printed material, such as TV programme SCHEDULES. MUSIC COPYRIGHT is very complex because any or all of the people involved in producing a commercial CD or other FORMAT may have rights. Licences can be obtained for copying and broadcasting copyright material, but you should always check with copyright holders.

CPU   Multimedia. The CPU is the Central Processing Unit of a computer. This is the chip that carries out multiple calculations and is at the heart of any computer.

CRAB   Sideways movement made by a TV STUDIO PEDESTAL camera or camera on a DOLLY. The operator moves the whole camera left or right. *See Crane, Pan, Track, Tilt Up/Down.*

CRANE   Counterweighted, long steel arm, with a flexible camera mounting that can be raised high above the set. Camera can TILT, PAN and ZOOM by remote control. Larger CAMERA CRANES employed in movies can carry a 35mm camera and CAMERA OPERATOR. *See Dolly, Track.*

Remote-controlled camera crane

CRANE SHOT   Shot taken from a camera CRANE, typically a HIGH-ANGLE SHOT.

CREDITS   List of people who have worked on, acted in and created a TV programme or film. Displayed at the end of the programme or film, and run over music, often with selected pictures. Television credits usually run for about 30 seconds and are typically created by a caption generator such as ASTON. Radio programmes only have full credits for drama. Factual programmes on talk stations, such as Radio 4, often have a PRODUCER and/or RESEARCHER credit read by the CONTINUITY ANNOUNCER. Modern films run long lists of credits, including the cast list and names of everybody from the humblest RUNNER to the CINEMATOGRAPHER. Many films use the credits as an opportunity to attach a commercial CD to the movie, as in James Cameron's *Titanic*, or to continue the story in a creative and amusing way, e.g. Robert Rodriguez's entertaining family film, *Spy Kids 2*, has the lead teenage actors fulfilling the dream of many young people by performing (miming) as rock stars in front of an adoring young audience. There is no need for credits to be boring!

CREW   Skilled technical personnel who make up the workforce on any media creation. Traditionally, in TV, the crew are the technical personnel who make sure everything happens *on* the day, and the PRODUCTION personnel make sure it happens *before* the day. In reality, both work together to create any professional media product.

CROP   Print. Describes the process of editing a photograph or piece of artwork so as to exclude any unwanted material and to keep the main subject in the centre of the FRAME. Photographs are cropped so they will fit on the page. Can be done physically with a scalpel and ruler. Most print publications use appropriate software on a computer, such as PHOTOSHOP.

CROSS-FADE   Audio. A slow transition from one sound source to another. Another term for an AUDIO MIX performed on a SOUND MIXING DESK. *See Fader, Transition, Dissolve.*

CROSSING THE LINE   Term used to describe how a SHOT has been filmed where the action seems to be reversed from the way it has been so far, or where a character seems to be looking the wrong side of the FRAME. Literally, means that the camera has crossed an invisible line that can be drawn between two or more interacting characters. By keeping to the same side of the line, the visual impression for the viewer that the characters are talking or relating to each other is preserved. To shoot the scene from the other side of the line will mean the EYELINES of the characters are not looking in the right directions, making the viewer confused and spoiling the seamless illusion of CONTINUITY.

CSO   Colour Separation Overlay. Another name for CHROMAKEY.

CU (CLOSE-UP)   Describes the size of SHOT of a person in the FRAME showing just the head, with the bottom of the frame just below the chin. CU of an object shows the object on its own and in isolation from anything else that may be visible in the WIDE SHOT. *See Shot Size, Close-up.*

CUE TV, film and radio.

a) Signal to an actor or presenter to start talking or moving, according to the SCRIPT or as prearranged. Can be a hand signal from a FLOOR MANAGER in a TV STUDIO or a flash of a green CUE LIGHT in a radio studio.

b) Signal to the operator to start a piece of equipment.

c) To cue or line up a video recorder, PLAYBACK machine or other equipment so that when it is activated it will start at exactly the right place, e.g. 'cue the video to play from the opening WIDE SHOT of a cross channel ferry leaving Dover'.

CUE LIGHT Radio. Light – often with a green bulb – in a radio STUDIO that can be switched on from the CONTROL ROOM. Gives the CONTRIBUTOR a visible sign when he or she should start to speak. *See Cue.*

CUE SHEET Document with details of a programme required by the broadcasting company in order to TRANSMIT that programme on the right day, at the right time and with the relevant CONTINUITY material. Includes the SCRIPT to be read by the CONTINUITY ANNOUNCER as a STUDIO introduction, e.g. 'And now for the fifth programme in our series about the paranormal. Here's Rory Thomson.' The cue sheet includes TX time, name and DURATION of programme, the exact opening and closing words that are on tape and the BACK ANNO. Also any other relevant material such as the EMAIL address or telephone number for a helpline for the topic of the programme.

CUKALORIS Lighting. Known as a cookie. Device to create projected light patterns or mottled light effects on a CYCLORAMA or other part of a film or TV set. Made of fine-mesh toughened cloth or plastic and perforated with a pattern of holes. Placed in front of a lamp, and used to soften a plain background or to make that part of the set more interesting. Density of the light pattern changes depending on the distance between the cookie and the lamp. Very close to the lamp, the effect will be soft and subtle. Further away, the mottling effect will be more pronounced. Invented for use in the US film industry. Originally cut out by hand from plywood by lighting operatives to create intricate and delicate patterns. *See GOBO*.

CUT

a) 'Cut' is the direction given to the cast and CREW to stop filming and to stop the ACTION during a TAKE on a film or TV set. Usually given by the DIRECTOR or First AD.

b) In EDITING, a cut is the sudden transition from one picture to another. On film, it means to literally make a cut at the join of one FRAME and add it to a different frame.

CUTAWAY On TV, a cutaway is a SHOT of something relevant to the content of an INTERVIEW, which is inserted into the shots of the person talking. Cutaways enhance the interview, which, otherwise would be just a TALKING HEAD, e.g. a pilot talking about flying faster than the speed of sound could have pictures of Concorde as cutaways. Cutaways give you the ability, in EDITING, to cut away from the CONTRIBUTOR at the point where you want to edit for content. Preferably, they are shots of what the contributor is talking about. The most common mistake inexperienced DIRECTORS make, is not to shoot enough cutaway material. You need much more than you think. Construct cutaways in visual sequences. You need different-sized shots for each sequence so that the sequences will cut together. A cutaway is inserted during editing to cover a **SOUND** edit in an interview that would otherwise be a **JUMP-CUT**. Without the cutaway, the head of the **INTERVIEWEE** would appear to jerk or jump where the **EDITOR** has edited a single shot of the interviewee talking. A TV studio **VISION MIXER** will cut away from one shot to another. Here, a cut is distinct from a **MIX** or **WIPE**. *See Gallery, Post-production.*

CUT-OFF   TV. The area around the edges of the TV **FRAME** that is not visible to the home viewer receiving pictures on a domestic television. When framing a **SHOT**, the **CAMERA OPERATOR** has to be aware of domestic cut-off and not include important visual information in the outside edges of the frame. Some professional cameras have the ability to show a safe cut-off area marked as a frame within a frame in the **VIEWFINDER**. Some broadcasters insist that when shooting in **WIDESCREEN**, the picture is composed so that all the **ACTION** is within an area of the frame that can be seen by viewers without a domestic widescreen television receiver.

CUTTING ORDER   Factual TV. Written list compiled by the **DIRECTOR** of the order in which the **SHOTS** and sequences in a TV programme or film should be cut together. Includes the in words, out words and relevant **TIME CODES** of each sequence of **DIALOGUE**. May include sections taken from the **TRANSCRIPT**. Given to the film/video **EDITOR**, at the beginning of an editing session, who will then compile a first **ASSEMBLY**. *See Online Edit, Offline Edit.*

CYBERSPACE   Internet. The apparent world of imaginary space that computer files fly through on the **WORLD WIDE WEB** or when using **EMAIL**. It is a way of explaining the complex area of how web pages are stored and how the information on the web reaches a user's computer.

CYCLORAMA (CYKE)   Large backing cloth or curtain, often on tracks (curtain rails), that can be pulled in front of the entire length of the back walls of the TV **STUDIO**, or that part of the studio being used as the set. When lit, can give the effect of a neutral or coloured background, with the illusion of making the studio look larger than it is. *See Ground Row.*

DAB Digital audio broadcasting. Pioneered by BBC Radio, DAB started in 1995 as a system of transmitting radio signals DIGITALLY. After a slow start, due to lack of affordable receivers, DAB began to take off in 2001 as the cost of tuners came down to about £100. Offers DISTORTION-free, crystal-clear radio reception, with near CD-quality SOUND and additional text/data information, such as name of station, disc playing, advertising and NEWS. New digital radio stations are now transmitting and virtually all national radio stations in the UK transmit digitally. The DAB system conforms to the European standard known as Eureka 147, which uses digital COMPRESSION to reduce the bit rate for each AUDIO source. Up to six stereo radio services can be MULTIPLEXED together, and a single FREQUENCY for each station can be used to cover the whole country.

DAILIES The rolls of FILM shot each day during the filming of a production. Known in the UK as RUSHES. The film is processed overnight and viewed in a viewing theatre with the sound. Often viewed on VHS by the DIRECTOR and the LIGHTING CAMERAMAN on the set the next day, or in the hotel at night. Used to check the QUALITY of the footage in terms of lighting, SOUND, CONTINUITY and performance of the actors.

DAT Digital Audio Tape. Extremely high-QUALITY, non-compressed DIGITAL sound recording system. SOUND is recorded by rotating heads onto a small CASSETTE DAT tape. Used in recording STUDIOS, radio PRODUCTION and on film and TV LOCATION shoots.

DAVE Radio. Proprietary software to EDIT sound DIGITALLY on a computer. Now superseded by COOL EDIT PRO.

DAY FOR NIGHT Filming SCENES set at night during daylight hours. A special FILTER is used on the camera to simulate night-time. With careful lighting, and by under-exposing the film, these scenes can be effective. A technique used by Hollywood B-feature filmmakers, in particular, to lower costs. Night work would involve the heavy extra payments for the CREW stipulated by the unions. Still used for saving money on TV drama and in some films. Generally fallen out of favour as being too stylised. Satirised in Francois Truffaut's 1973 film, *La Nuit Américaine*, the term used by the French to describe day-for-night filming.

dB *See Decibel.*

DEADLINE Time and date at which anything to do with media dissemination, such as a print ARTICLE, piece for radio, SCRIPT, film or TV programme, must be delivered for TRANSMISSION or printing. Any other agreed delivery time. Deadlines are many and varied, depending on the **SCHEDULE** of any **PRODUCTION**. Most TV programmes have deadlines for each stage of the work, such as the completion of filming before going on to **POST-PRODUCTION**.

DECIBEL (dB)   A measure of the relative intensity or loudness of **SOUND**. Works on a logarithmic law and is not an absolute value, but a measurement of comparison. *See **Dynamic Range, Microphone.***

DEPRESS   Instruction to a video **CAMERA OPERATOR** on a **PEDESTAL** camera. Means to decrease the height of the camera by lowering the camera on the pedestal.

DEPTH OF FIELD   Relates to still and moving-image photography and video camerawork. Depth of field is the area in the **FRAME**, both in front of and behind the point you actually **FOCUS** on, that is crystal clear and also in focus. The depth of field depends on the **FOCAL LENGTH** of the **LENS** and the **APERTURE** setting or **F-STOP**. *See **Iris and Focus.***

DESIGNER   Person responsible for designing and supervising the building of the set for a TV **STUDIO** show. Also known as the production designer on a film. Adapts and 'dresses' **LOCATIONS** for drama or for an **OUTSIDE BROADCAST**. Important member of the production team for any period drama or film that wants an original or stylish look. Also known as the art director on a feature film. On a sci-fi or fantasy film, responsible for creating a whole believable world that will draw an **AUDIENCE** in and provide the setting for the characters and **ACTION**, e.g. the *Harry Potter* films.

DESKTOP PUBLISHING (DTP)   Print. Generic term for creating a print publication on a computer using suitable software. It is possible to publish from a desktop computer or go directly onto the internet, with text and images, including photographs, graphic design and page set-ups using dedicated software such as PhotoShop. Professional publications generally use QuarkXpress.

DEVELOPMENT   Refers to the time spent by a film **PRODUCER**, writer or a **PRODUCTION** company in setting up a film project. Can be weeks, months or years. Large movie **STUDIOS** can and do provide development finance for what they think is a good idea. This can mean a number of rewrites for the **SCRIPT** and time to interest a star actor in the project. It can also allow time to seek more money to make the movie. For smaller projects, a few weeks in development can mean time to finalise **CONTRACTS** and get a fully realisable **SCREENPLAY**. In television development, time often has to be financed by an **INDEPENDENT PRODUCER** for his or her own project, so that it can be **PITCHED** at a broadcaster.

DIALOGUE   The spoken words from a drama **SCRIPT**. Literally, means verbal interaction between two people, but dialogue has come to mean any speech between two or more characters or even just the words of one character alone. The dialogue drives many scripts, as it gives life to the characters and can invigorate the plot. Writing a **SCREENPLAY** for a film involves more than just the dialogue between characters. The visual storytelling is what really attracts an **AUDIENCE**, as well as slick and naturalistic dialogue.

DIEGETIC   Comes from the Greek word meaning narrative, but nearly always refers to

SOUND. Diegetic sound is sound material that relates to the SCENE and is recorded – or appears to be recorded – at the same time as the DIALOGUE or ACTION in a scene. This recorded sound is therefore part of the narrative of the scene. For example the singing of birds recorded in the background of an EXTERIOR dialogue scene would be diegetic sound. Non-diegetic sound is added afterwards in POST-PRODUCTION, and is extraneous to the narrative of the scene. The most common example of non-diegetic sound is the music added to a film that is part of the SOUNDTRACK but clearly extraneous to the action.

DIFFUSION   Lighting. A way of varying the intensity of a light source and making it SOFTER by using a diffuser. A diffuser is translucent material that is fixed over the front of a lamp to soften highlights, reduce contrast and increase the spread of light from the lamp.

DIGI BETA   *See Digital Betacam.*

DIGITAL   Data – could be text, artwork, SOUND, or video pictures – that are represented in digital or binary form as a series of electronic pulses. The basis of the computer. The term digital refers to the fingers and thumbs used in ancient times for counting and is associated with whole numbers. Digital technology is binary (means two); it records data using only two numbers, one and zero. In electronic circuits, this means that switches are either on or off, and there is no confusion or halfway house. To make a number or value greater than one, combinations of binary digits are used. These are called BITS. So, two bits give four possible combinations: 00, 01, 10, 11. Eight bits are known as one BYTE, which is 256 different combinations of ones and zeros. The value of digital technology is that there are no variables, unlike ANALOGUE technology. Crucially, digital technology provides AUDIO and video recording with no noise or distortion and no loss of QUALITY. The process is called SAMPLING and consists of measuring the voltage of an electrical signal at a large number of discrete points in time in order to recreate it in binary from. Digital recordings can be copied an infinite number of times with no loss of quality or RESOLUTION. Digital technology is now the basis for most of the media industry – cameras, video, SOUND, MULTIMEDIA, the internet and digital broadcasting.

DIGITAL BETACAM (DIGI BETA)   Sony DIGITAL camcorder, providing very high broadcast-QUALITY pictures and SOUND, storing the digital data onto digital tape. Apart from IIDTV, Digi Beta is one of the highest technical-quality video-recording systems used in television and video work. *See Compression, Digital Editing, Format.*

DIGITAL CAMERA   Photography and video. Generally refers to a still camera that records pictures on CCD rather than on celluloid film. A matrix of very small sensors converts light into electrical signals and into a grid of coloured squares called PIXELS. The pixels adjust the colour and sharpness to make up the image. The definition, or QUALITY, of the picture, is called RESOLUTION and depends on the number of pixels that make up the image. A camera's resolution determines how the pictures will look when they are printed and what can be done with them once they are on the computer. A digital camera, with a resolution of at least three million pixels, is needed to give photo-quality prints. The image is stored digitally using COMPRESSION, either in the camera or on a removable memory card or memory stick.

Popular memory card storage formats include CompactFlash and SmartMedia. A 16-Mb CompactFlash card typically stores up to 160 pictures. Video camcorders store the data on a **VIDEOTAPE** format, such as **DIGITAL BETACAM** or **DV**. Digital cameras have a cable to download the image data onto a computer, either through a serial or **USB** connection. Moving images are best transferred using the fast **FIREWIRE** connection. Some modern cameras have an infrared system to connect the camera to the computer. Most digital cameras have all the features of a traditional film camera, such as a built-in flash and **ZOOM** lens. Additional features include an **LCD** panel, to view the pictures before you take them and to review them afterwards. Some digital still cameras have a mini-video or 'burst' mode that can take three or more pictures per second. Video camcorders have most of these facilities. Websites that have more information about digital photography include www.steves-digicams.com and www.dpreview.com.

DIGITAL EDITING   **DIGITAL** editing is now universal in TV and radio as the preferred form of **NON-LINEAR EDITING**. This can be **OFFLINE** or **ONLINE**. Dedicated software such as **AVID**, **ADOBE PREMIERE** or **FINAL CUT PRO** can **DIGITISE** pictures and **SOUND** into a computer, where they can be assembled in any order on a **TIMELINE**. **DISSOLVES** and other **TRANSITIONS** can be added and sophisticated visual effects created, including **CHROMAKEY**. DV digital recordings can be played straight into a digital editing system through a **FIREWIRE**

Digital editing

or iLink. The edited pictures and sound can be laid back out of the computer onto digital tape, without any loss of picture or sound QUALITY. Digital editing in radio works in the same way and displays on the computer screen the original sound signal as a wave form – double wave form for stereo – so that it can be edited. *See Cool Edit Pro, SADiE.*

DIGITAL RECORDING   The recording of SOUND and pictures by a DIGITAL process so that only binary data is stored on disc or tape. To record sound digitally involves SAMPLING the signal and recording binary data onto a digital format such as DV, DIGITAL BETACAM, DAT or MINIDISC. *See Digital, Compression, Sampling, VCR.*

DIGITAL THEATRE SYSTEM (DTS)   Audio. High-quality DIGITAL surround-sound SOUNDTRACK that is available on some films on DVD. *See Dolby.*

DIGITAL TV

a) Generic name for the DIGITAL TRANSMISSION and often production of broadcast television channels in the UK and US.

b) A digital TV is a television receiver that has a built-in decoder and can pick up digital broadcasts.

DIGITAL ZOOM   Way of making the subject larger in the FRAME of a DIGITAL CAMERA. The camera enlarges the centre area digitally. The quality is not likely to be as good as using an optical ZOOM lens.

DIGITISE   To convert an ANALOGUE signal into a DIGITAL form as a series of electronic impulses that can be stored in a computer. Used to transfer data such as video pictures from a camcorder or VCR into a computer for video EDITING. Once the material is digitised, it can be manipulated by the editing software. *See Avid, Adobe Premiere, Compression, Digital, Sampling.*

DIOPTER LENS   Refers to a LENS that can be added onto the main lens on a camera to alter its FOCAL LENGTH. One reason to do this is to reduce the effective focal length of the lens so that it can focus on a subject that is closer than normal.

DirectMusic   Multimedia. Part of DirectX, Microsoft's interface software that enables games to run on the Windows platform. DirectMusic extends the possibilities of MIDI, so that every part of the music – the pitch, DURATION of the note and its SOUND – can be changed as the music plays. Microsoft's Xbox video games console has hardware that will accelerate DirectMusic without compromising other system resources. *See DLS.*

DIRECTOR

a) Director in factual television works alongside the PRODUCER and is responsible for the overall look and much of the content of a TV programme. Does the RESEARCH, films CONTRIBUTORS, creates an ASSEMBLY ORDER, supervises EDITING and is responsible for delivering the final programme.

b) Director in TV drama is responsible for interpreting the SCRIPT and staging the production visually. Directs actors in movement, ACTION sequences and delivery of DIALOGUE. Works with the LIGHTING CAMERAMAN to set up SHOT SIZE, camera ANGLE and camera movement to reveal the content of a SCENE. AUDITIONS actors, creates a

STORYBOARD, liaises with the production manager over SCHEDULES and BUDGETS. Works with PRODUCTION and CREW to achieve SPECIAL EFFECTS, stunts and make everything that appears on the screen happen at the right time. Is responsible for the look, pace, feel, structure and style created in the editing of a drama.

c) FILM DIRECTOR is responsible for all the above and absolutely everything to do with the look, shape and content of a feature film. From working on the script to the final edit, the film director is in complete control; the only thing he probably has no control over are the film's finances, which are the province of the PRODUCER.

DIRECTOR OF PHOTOGRAPHY (DOP)   The way a character is lit, and the mood and style of lighting of the SET are down to the DOP. Works closely with the DIRECTOR in visualising a filmed drama, commercial or music promo. Generally works on 35mm or super 16mm film or HD video. Expert on technical side with strong creative artistic sensibility. Particularly concerned with the lighting. Responsible for the CAMERA OPERATOR, GRIP and the ASSISTANT CAMERAMAN. Chooses the FILM STOCK, selects camera LENSES and will FRAME the SHOTS. On smaller shoots, known as LIGHTING CAMERAMAN, and on a feature film may be called the CINEMATOGRAPHER.

DIRECTORS' GUILD OF GREAT BRITAIN   Acorn House, 314–320 Gray's Inn Road, London WC1X 8DP www.dggb.co.uk Represents the interests of directors working in film, television and theatre and throughout the media in the UK.

DIRECTORY   Internet. A website that lists vast numbers of other websites, categorised under subject headings, themes and other simple-to-use categories. Much more than a sophisticated telephone directory, but not quite as sophisticated as a SEARCH ENGINE. Best-known example is www.yahoo.com.

DISSOLVE   Film and video EDITING. The gradual merging and replacing of one image, or SHOT, with another. Can be quite short or over several seconds. Created in editing. *See Transition.*

DISTORTION   Refers to the way an AUDIO and video signal can change in a way that alters it for the worse from the original, e.g. when an incoming audio signal becomes too loud for the recording set-up and goes over the limit on a recorder, it distorts and sounds fuzzy.

DLS   Multimedia. Downloadable synthesiser. Standard defined by Yamaha that allows musicians to DOWNLOAD their own SOUNDS into a computer SAMPLE memory. This allows for consistent PLAYBACK quality and tone when using a MIDI system.

D-NOTICE   Government guidelines that advise broadcasters and the press not to publish material that could be a threat to national security. Now more properly known as Defence Advisory Notices, they detail the categories of information where further guidance is needed. They are not imposed by the government, but issued by the Defence, Press and Broadcasting Advisory Committee. This is made up of senior civil servants and representatives of the press and broadcasting organisations. Although the issuing of a D-notice has no legal force, if ignored by a journalist it could mean a breach of the OFFICIAL SECRETS ACT.

DOCUDRAMA A programme that mixes drama and DOCUMENTARY by taking authenticated, real-life, topical or historical events and using actors and a drama SCRIPT to convey the situations and characters. Can be integrated with INTERVIEWS with genuine contributors, or may be pure drama.

DOCUMENTARY A factual radio or TV programme that examines, or documents, events, people and situations in the real world, using authentic non-fictional material. It has come to mean a serious film or programme based on hard evidence and good RESEARCH. The term documentary is generally considered to have been invented by the filmmaker, John Grierson, in about 1926. Grierson had definite ideas about what a documentary should do. He believed it must be more than a film providing evidence or information about the socio-economic world. It should use a whole range of creative skills to fashion 'fragments of reality' into a film, which has a specific social, educational and cultural impact. He believed a documentary should be a 'creative treatment of actuality' with a clearly defined social purpose. Ever since, there has been a debate on how much creativity should go into the making of a documentary and how transparent this should be.

DOLBY DIGITAL Audio. Dolby is a trade name for a complex noise suppression system on AUDIO systems and on film or video SOUNDTRACKS. It is also a surround-sound system used in cinemas and on DVDs. *See Digital Theatre System.*

DOLLY General term for a wheeled mounting for a camera, allowing the camera to move with the ACTION. There are many types of dolly, ranging from the quite simple – just the camera on a wheeled TRIPOD – to larger mountings that can hold the camera, CAMERA OPERATOR and a FOCUS PULLER. A typical film camera dolly runs on specially laid tracks. This allows the camera to take steady, smooth shots, known as TRACKING SHOTS, that move in or out from a subject, without the use of the ZOOM, and allows it to move around a subject or TRACK with a moving subject. *See Crab, Crane, Pan, Tilt Up/Down.*

DOLLY IN To move the camera, which is mounted on any sort of DOLLY, in towards the subject of the scene.

DOLLY OUT To move the camera, which is mounted on a DOLLY, away from the subject. A film dolly would be on tracks and give a smooth, carefully controlled, moving SHOT out from the subject. Can be a complex move, if the camera needs to keep the subject in FOCUS and there are low levels of light. An ASSISTANT CAMERAMAN may need to PULL FOCUS. In a TV STUDIO, it is a request from the DIRECTOR to the operator of a PEDESTAL CAMERA to move back from the subject.

DOMAIN Internet. That part of a website address that identifies it as unique. Typically, has the name of the site followed by a domain category such as .org or .com, followed by the country, e.g. .uk. That domain can then be identified and located on the internet, as no two websites can have the same domain address. The rapid spread of internet communications, and the proliferation of companies setting up on the internet in the last ten years of the twentieth century, was named the .com (dotcom) revolution.

DOORSTEPPING   Waiting all day, and all night if necessary, on or near the place (doorstep) where a politician or other important person is staying, in order to get an INTERVIEW for press or broadcasting. Newspaper journalists are probably best known for doorstepping celebrities to try to get a scoop.

DOTS PER INCH (dpi)   Refers to the number of dots per inch used to print a photograph or piece of artwork. Used when comparing the print quality or RESOLUTION of a computer PRINTER or SCANNER. Generally, the larger the dpi, the better the quality of the print.

DOUBLE PAGE SPREAD   Print. A feature article in a MAGAZINE that runs over two pages that are facing each other, usually with photograph(s) and headings. *See Copy, Centrespread.*

DOWNLOAD   Multimedia. Copying or transferring a web page from the internet onto a user's computer. Not just text material, but whole software packages, music files, video, artwork and photographs can all be downloaded with suitable software. Most material on the web can be downloaded, from a photo of Madonna to the entire works of Shakespeare, but check for COPYRIGHT.

DOWNSTAGE   Term from the theatre used on TV dramas and films that refers to that part of the ACTION that is nearest to the camera. Often used as an instruction to scenery CREW: 'Move that chair a couple of metres downstage.'

dpi   Print. *See Dots Per Inch.*

Dreamweaver   Multimedia. Trade name for Macromedia software package to develop a professional website with comprehensive visual LAYOUT tools and text-editing environment. Version 4 allows Macromedia Flash graphics to be directly input to Dreamweaver. There are two main software packages used for creating web pages: Microsoft Frontpage and Macromedia Dreamweaver.

DROPOUT   An audible or visual 'hole' in the tape of a recorded video or sound INTERVIEW. On sound there is a moment of silence, and on videotape a FRAME or two appears not to have recorded properly and has DISTORTION lines. Can be short horizontal lines that appear intermittently or small white dots on the screen. Caused by impurities or damage in the oxide coating of the VIDEOTAPE.

DRY-HIRE   The hiring of AUDIO and TV facilities and kit without the use of a professional operator, e.g. the hiring of an AVID editing suite that can be operated by yourself or an editor that you choose. Dry-hire covers many facilities for media production, from the rent of a TV STUDIO space with no personnel for a day, to the monthly hire of a TRIPOD and camcorder. There are many companies all over the world offering dry-hire. In London, many of them are based around the Soho area.

DRY RUN   Complete run-through of a TV or radio show before TRANSMISSION, to check that everything goes well, rather like a dress rehearsal. Can be with or without technical staff and facilities, such as cameras and MICROPHONES. *See TV Studio, Talent.*

DTRS   Digital Tape Recording System. Proprietary high-quality AUDIO recording system by electronics company Tascam. Records onto 8mm tape with up to 120 tracks.

DUB

a) Literally, means to copy.

b) In programme production, means to blend or mix together the AUDIO elements of the production. Using a sophisticated SOUND MIXING DESK, speech, ACTUALITY, music and SOUND FX, and maybe COMMENTARY, are mixed and BALANCED to create the STEREO SOUNDTRACK.

c) The dub is shorthand for the time spent DUBBING or the place where the dub is located, e.g. where is the dub today?

DUBBING

The process of mixing and BALANCING all the different AUDIO elements in a TV programme or film. Comes from a film industry term meaning to copy. This is where the tracks with DIALOGUE, ACTUALITY, music, COMMENTARY and SOUND FX are mixed on a SOUND MIXING DESK to create the final soundtrack for a programme. In the case of a modern feature film, such as Baz Lurhman's *Moulin Rouge*, this can be extremely complex and take many months. ***See Dubbing Theatre, M & E, Track Lay.***

DUBBING THEATRE

The place where a sound DUB happens. Has a sophisticated SOUND MIXING DESK. Video PLAYBACK is projected onto a large screen. Modern theatres are all DIGITAL and use computer EDITING software to set up and 'lay' the AUDIO tracks. COMMENTARY can be added or SPOT SOUND FX created to add to the MIX. The production team can hear the mixed sound played back with the pictures at each stage, and suggest modifications if necessary. A straightforward 30-minute TV factual programme can take about a day (eight to ten hours) to dub, if all goes well!

DUMMY

Print. Mock-up of how a printed page, book cover or any printed material will look when it has been printed. May not contain all the COPY and may leave blank rectangular shapes to show where the artwork or advertisements will be. Colours and TYPE size may be negotiable. ***See Bleed, Layout.***

DURATION

The exact length in minutes and seconds of a TV or radio programme or film, often written as DUR.

DV

Digital Video. DIGITAL video recording format family that covers MINI-DV, DVCAM, DVC and DVCPRO. Widely adopted as the professional standard in television programme acquisition. Records onto a small CASSETTE of metal evaporated tape that is carbon coated for strength. Very good-QUALITY pictures. Has taken over as the preferred FORMAT for consumer camcorders and non-drama LOCATION broadcast TV. Especially popular for DOCUMENTARIES and other factual programmes, due to the compact size of the cameras. Only limitation, DV is not recommended for CHROMAKEY. Pictures can be downloaded via FIREWIRE or via a USB link for NON-LINEAR EDITING on a computer. Suitable professional video editing packages include AVID Xpress DV, FINAL CUT PRO and ADOBE PREMIERE. The advantage of using these systems is that there is no distinction between OFFLINE and ONLINE EDITING. Using an IEEE 1394 or Firewire link, all editing is the same quality as the original. Most DV camcorders come with a suitable Firewire socket allowing use of the camcorder as the play-in deck.

Operating a DV camera

DVD   Digital Versatile Disc. Video **PLAYBACK** and recording **FORMAT**. A 12cm plastic disc that can play back (some can record), very high-quality pictures and sound. A DVD can hold up to eight hours of video, and potentially over 50 hours of excellent **QUALITY AUDIO**; that's 18 **GIGABYTES** of **DIGITAL** information. Available since 1997, the format is set to overtake **VHS** as the preferred format for renting and viewing feature films at home. Over 43 million players have been sold worldwide. DVD can work as a cross-platform format, can handle on-screen text and has **INTERACTIVE** functionality. Already, a newer DVD type of technology is becoming available, known as blue laser technology, offering improved performance.

DVD-R   DVD-recordable. High-**QUALITY** video recording that has taken the place of **VHS** recording. Also known as **DVD-RAM, DVD+RW**. Not nearly as expensive as they were. Creates an image index of what is recorded on the disc, for easy search and near-instant access. **DVD** recording machines are available that can record on discs once only (DVD-R) or on discs that can be reused many times (DVD+RW). *See **DVD+R and DVD+RW.***

DVD+R   Newer DVD format. Faster and more technically advanced than DVD-R format. Excellent picture and SOUND quality. Over 80 per cent of standard DVD players can read these discs. Records onto write-once discs. For re-recordable discs, *see DVD+RW*.

DVD-RAM   Recordable DVD format used in computer drives, mainly for data storage. On this FORMAT, the discs may not play back in many standard DVD players. Now being superseded by DVD+R format.

DVD-RAM/R   Recordable FORMAT based on the DVD system, but recording onto a mini 8cm DVD disc that is write-once. Will play back in almost all standard DVD players.

DVD-ROM   Version of DVD used to store digital data. Offers higher-quality SOUND and larger storage capacity than CD-ROM.

DVD+RW   DVD system that records onto re-recordable discs. Standard recorders can record up to two hours of standard DVD-QUALITY video on each disc, or four hours of VHS-quality recording. Some recorders can record up to six hours of VHS-quality material. DVD+RW or DVD+R can be installed in the place of the CD drive in a computer. Will store large amounts of data or record video that has been edited on the computer. Most units will burn AUDIO and video CDs as well as DVDs.

DVE   Digital Visual Effects. Usually refers to a digital image switcher, located in a TV GALLERY or EDIT SUITE that can create and mix visual effects, such as a WIPE or flip for a TV programme.

DYNAMIC RANGE   Sound. The difference between the loudest and the quietest sounds measured in DECIBELS. In terms of human hearing, this ranges from about 15–20dB, which could be a very quiet remote woodland, to a low-flying jet aircraft, at about 120–125dB.

EARPIECE   Customised **AUDIO** device, similar to a single headphone, that fits snugly and unobtrusively into the ear of a **PRESENTER**. In a **TV STUDIO**, linked to the **TALKBACK** system, allowing the presenter to hear instructions from the studio **DIRECTOR**, but without hearing all the instructions to other members of the **CREW**. This is known as **SWITCHED TALKBACK**.

E-BOOK   Multimedia. A book that's been changed into a **DIGITAL** format, which can be easily and swiftly downloaded through the internet. Requires e-reader software to be accessible on a home computer. Some people query the value of this use of the internet.

EDITING   The process in film and TV of selecting and juxtaposing different images and **SOUNDS**, to tell a factual or fictitious story, create dramatic tension and express meaning.
a) TV editing is either **LINEAR** or **NON-LINEAR**.
b) In its simplest form, film editing is cutting **FRAMES** of film from the **RUSHES** and sticking them together with transparent tape to create a **ROUGH CUT**, or early version, of a programme.
c) Editing for TV and radio is now mainly non-linear and **DIGITAL**, and is done with a computer, coming under the process of **POST-PRODUCTION**. *See Adobe Premiere, Avid, Final Cut Pro.*
d) Editing in radio, up until the 1990s, involved the actual cutting with a razor blade of ¼-inch magnetic tape, on which was recorded the speech and sounds. Radio editing is now done digitally, on a computer package such as **COOL EDIT PRO** or **SADiE**.

EDITOR

a) TV, film. The person who assembles and puts together, in a narrative sequence, all the various **SCENES** and **SOUNDS** for a film, or TV programme. The editor usually works with the **DIRECTOR**, who prepares notes to create a first **ASSEMBLY** of the material. This is then revised and refined with the director to become a final cut. The film or video editor is also responsible for **TRACK LAYING** the sound leading up to the sound **DUB**.
b) Broadcast TV/radio. The person who is in overall charge of a TV or radio programme, or series of programmes, or of the day's news **OUTPUT**.
c) Print. The person who decides policy and is responsible for overall content of a newspaper or other print publications. In print, the editor can have considerable freedom over content and to hire and fire journalistic staff, or change and adapt the design and style of the publication. The editor will be most concerned with content, and can be instrumental in

increasing the circulation or turning round a flagging title by selecting the most eye-catching stories of the day.

EDIT SUITE   The location with the associated kit where **AUDIO** or video **EDITING** happens. Can refer to a small cubicle that just has a computer for **DIGITAL** editing and audio- or video-recording equipment. Can be a sophisticated, high-end editing suite located in a **FACILITY HOUSE**, with a wide range of digital equipment capable of creating **CGA** and employing advanced **POST-PRODUCTION** techniques.

EDL   Edit Decision List. Video. A list of the **TIME CODE** numbers, indicating the exact **LOCATION** of all edit points created during a video edit. The EDL is a list of all the in **FRAMES** and out frames for each sequence, and all the **AUDIO** cut points of a video programme. These have been selected by the **EDITOR** in the latest **ASSEMBLY**. On a computer editing system, the EDL is created automatically with each edit and as part of the **NON-LINEAR EDITING** process. Where an EDL has been created as part of an **OFFLINE EDIT**, it can be taken into an **EDIT SUITE** to be conformed. This is the process where the list of numbers (EDL) is turned back into edited pictures, usually in a semi-automated operation. A computer searches for each edit from the **RUSHES**, records the selected sequence on to a **VCR**, and so builds up the final programme tape, sequence by sequence. An EDL can be created manually with **LINEAR EDITING**.

EFFECTS BANK   Panel of switches and/or buttons used by the **VISION MIXER** on the **VISION MIXING DESK** in a **TV STUDIO** control **GALLERY**, which creates a variety of electronically generated visual effects, e.g. a **BOX WIPE**.

ELEMACK   Trade name for a particular lightweight camera **DOLLY**.

ELEVATE   Instruction to a video **CAMERA OPERATOR** on a **PEDESTAL** camera. Means to increase the height of the camera by raising the camera on the pedestal.

EMAIL   Multimedia. Electronic mail. Makes it possible to communicate with another email user, anywhere in the world, in a few seconds, via the internet. Has transformed international communications. Pictures, maps, diagrams and photographs can be scanned into the computer, electronically attached to an email, and sent across the world in an instant. Computer files can also be attached and sent with a message. Most **ISPs** provide free email addresses and an email service.

EMBARGO   A ban on a **NEWS** item or commercial information to prevent it being discussed in the press and in public. There is usually a date and time after which a news or other **ITEM**, or commercial promotion, can be discussed or aired in the media. During this period, the item is 'embargoed'.

EMOTICON   Multimedia. Keyboard shorthand to convey an idea. An emoticon tends to be a way of describing a facial expression and is made with certain keystrokes. These can suggest an image of a face sideways, e.g. a kiss is: (:-* and a smile is: :-) and you can – allegedly – ask for a dozen roses with: 12x@>--->--

ENCRYPTION   Multimedia. Means to send data in a coded form over the internet so that only the intended recipient can decipher and read the data.

END BOARD   In filmmaking, it is normal to show a **CLAPPERBOARD** on the front of a **TAKE** before the **ACTION** in the **SCENE** begins. Sometimes, the **DIRECTOR** will have reasons to put it at the end. In this case, the board is shown upside down, to indicate it is at the end of the take and not at the beginning, where the editor would expect to find it.

ENG   Electronic **NEWS** Gathering. Refers to the acquisition of TV news footage on **LOCATION** by video camcorder.

EQUITY   Union for all actors and other stage and media performers in the UK. Has agreements with UK broadcasters, regarding minimum daily rates, hours of work, pay and conditions. Offers advice and information on all aspects of working as a performer in the industry.

ESTABLISHING SHOT   A **SCENE**-setting **SHOT** that establishes the **LOCATION**, and possibly time and season, in which the subsequent scene, or sequence, or even the whole film, will take place. The opening shot in a Bond movie might be an aerial view, establishing a city or country, often with a **CAPTION** giving its name and the date in which the opening action takes place, e.g. a **WIDE SHOT** across the Thames of Big Ben and the Houses of Parliament, with a **PAN** across the London skyline to the east. Caption says: 'London, 2003'. This

Establishing shot

establishes a location that gives the film some of its dramatic thrust. A more modest establishing shot can be used in a short TV ITEM to show where a story is located. This could be a wide shot of the park in Ealing, West London, where a skateboarding duck sometimes entertains the park visitors. *See Shot Size.*

EXECUTIVE PRODUCER   The person in overall charge of a strand, series or department in television and radio broadcasting, e.g. comedy in both ITV and the BBC has an executive producer. Main function of an executive producer in film is to raise finance or put in some of their own money. Not concerned with the practical making of the film. *See Film Producer, Producer.*

EXPENSES   All media. The money that can be claimed back, usually from the PRODUCTION company, for travel and other expenses incurred while on LOCATION or away from base. Traditionally seen as a 'creative' way to boost income, but in the modern climate of fiscal control in the media industry, it seems to be increasingly difficult to claim back what is actually owed. It is essential to retain all receipts for travel, food and accommodation. *See Per Diem.*

EXPOSURE   Photography. Literally, exposure is the amount of light allowed to reach the raw FILM STOCK in a camera. This is crucial, as it determines whether the moving or still image will be too dark, too light or perfectly exposed. Cameras have the ability to adjust and set the APERTURE and the SHUTTER to produce the correct amount of light needed to take well-defined pictures on film or DIGITALLY in any conditions. Sometimes, if the light is difficult or the conditions unusual, it is better to manually override the AUTO-EXPOSURE and make your own settings. To balance manual settings, for either aperture or shutter, is known as exposure compensation.

EXTERIOR (EXT.)   TV, film, video. Describes the LOCATION for a SCENE as being outside, often with the sky or sun as the means of illumination. This is as opposed to inside a building, studio or other edifice that needs to be lit artificially, which is marked as INTERIOR. Used in a SCRIPT to denote where the action takes place, e.g. Exterior Waterloo Station. Used in a STORYBOARD or SHOOTING SCRIPT to tell the CREW and cast that the scene will be set outside – hopefully in the fresh air and sunlight – or that the shot needs to be taken from the outside of a building, e.g. a scripted scene could start with: EXT. garden. Lit downstairs window. The alien looks through the window to see the family watching television.

EXTRA   Non-speaking and non-featured role in a film or TV drama. Can be directed in terms of moves and actions. Cannot speak lines or be more than a member of a crowd. Can make crowd noises. An extra is paid less than a WALK-ON.

EYELINE   TV, film, video. In setting up a SHOT for any moving-image project, it is vital that the eyeline of a character – the direction in which the eyes are looking – matches the eyeline of the character he or she is talking to. If the character looks across the room and catches someone's eye, it is vital that the direction of the eyes on the CLOSE-UP shot matches that on a WIDE SHOT. In a simple scenario of a person on a horse talking to someone standing at street level, the character on the horse must be seen to look down and towards the position of the street character. This eyeline must be particularly carefully set up for the **CU** shot, and **CONTINUITY** kept for all the other shots. In more complex set-ups, the eyelines of all characters have to be very carefully matched to maintain cinematic credulity.

FACILITY FEE   A sum of money paid to an individual or company for the use of premises or other LOCATION, or for facilities required by a production company. Payments vary according to the desirability and size of the premises or to the particular facility that is provided. A stately home owned by the National Trust will cost upwards of £1000 a day, but a modest modern apartment will cost a lot less. Somebody might lend their model railway for a scene in a TV drama, and for this a facility fee could be paid. *See Contract, Contributor's Agreement, Release Form.*

FACILITY HOUSE   Commercial company offering a range of TV and/or film facilities for hire. Usually ONLINE and OFFLINE EDITING and other production facilities for hire to production companies. Some facility houses just offer EDITING equipment that can be hired by the hour, day, week or longer, with and without an experienced EDITOR. Other facility houses, such as The Mill in London, offer very sophisticated, high-end DIGITAL kit, with highly skilled operators to create computer-generated imaging (CGI) for movies and TV.

FACTUAL PROGRAMMING   TV or radio programmes across a whole range of genres that are based on real people and real events, with no element of FICTION. Term used to differentiate these programmes from other areas of broadcast output such as NEWS, entertainment and drama programming. *See Documentary.*

FADE IN

a) Term used in picture editing or VISION MIXING. Refers to the way one picture gradually comes into vision, often from a black screen or from a title sequence. Used in a SCRIPT at the start of a movie where an ESTABLISHING SHOT is faded in from the opening credit sequence.

b) In sound editing, refers to the way one sound is gradually added to or replaces another. In radio, music is often faded in under speech. It comes in at a very low volume and then increases to the normal level as the speech finishes. See FADER.

FADE OUT

a) Term used in picture editing or VISION MIXING. Refers to the way a picture gradually disappears from the screen, usually leaving a moment of black. Often used to denote the passage of time. Also, at the end of a CREDITS sequence in TV or movies, where the screen fades to black, denoting the end of the film. *See Gallery, Post-production.*

b) In sound editing, refers to the way one sound is gradually taken out of the sound mix, by moving the FADER down. In radio, music is often faded out at the end of a recording or disc.

This makes for a smoother transition to speech or to the next piece of music, or to denote the end of the programme. ***See Audio Mixer, Dub, Dubbing, Fader, Sound.***

FADER   Slide volume or gain control. Used in sound **EDITING** on a **SOUND MIXING DESK** to mix one sound source with another, or alter the level (**VOLUME**) of a selected sound source, e.g. **MICROPHONE**. Also used as a picture control lever on a **VISION MIXING DESK**, to bring up or **FADE IN** a picture, or at the end of a programme to **FADE OUT** the picture altogether to a black screen.

FEATURE

a) Radio. A feature is the name given to an important **ITEM** in a **MAGAZINE** programme, or as shorthand for a feature programme. This is a programme that is primarily about a particular subject or person, e.g. a feature on Saddam Hussein or a feature on greenhouse gases.

b) Print. A major **ARTICLE** or **STORY** in a publication that is more in-depth than a normal article. Can be based around an **INTERVIEW** with a well-known person, or a journalistic piece involving considerable research.

c) Film. Shorthand for **FEATURE FILM**.

FEATURE FILM   Describes a full-length commercial film, i.e. a movie shown in a cinema to a paying **AUDIENCE**. Officially, has to be over 34 minutes or it is classified as a **SHORT**. Most feature films are at least 90 minutes and may last more than three hours.

FEEDBACK

a) Name given to the response from the **AUDIENCE** to a media product. Can be written, **EMAILED**, given over the phone or in a special programme, requesting information or offering criticism, and occasionally praise, to a broadcast radio or TV programme, or from readers to a print publication in a letters page.

b) Sound. Acoustic or electrical feedback is the very nasty loud noise made when a sound is fed back into a **SPEAKER** causing **HOWL-ROUND**. Often heard in public address systems as a high-pitched whine when the **MICROPHONE** picks up noise from the speaker system, which is then amplified back through the speakers.

c) Working in a recording studio, feedback is a way of feeding the output of a recording machine back into the input of the same or another recording machine to create a particular effect, such as an echo.

FICTIONAL NAMES   In fictional drama, the scriptwriter invents names for characters. When the **SCRIPT** comes into production, these names have to be checked against a number of registers. A fictional full name cannot be directly related to any particular living person. There are only so many first names, and writers working on realistic modern plots will want to use current first names. It is putting it together with a family name that could create the name of a living person and cause the production company to be taken to court. There are likely to be many John Smiths, but the writer has to be careful that no one John Smith can be identified by the fictional characterisation. Better to try and choose less obvious combinations; even so, they must be checked.

FIELD PRODUCER   TV producer or director working on **LOCATION** with editorial responsibilities, usually working in **NEWS** and current affairs.

FILE   Multimedia. Data that is named and stored in a computer.

   Print. A journalist will file **COPY** to the newspaper for which he or she is writing. Means to send the copy electronically, by fax or by phone, for inclusion in the next edition.

FILL LIGHT   Film and TV lighting. The fill light is used in conjunction with a **KEY LIGHT** to 'fill in' the darker areas that the key light has not reached and to reduce contrast. It is usually a soft, diffused or reflected light. Usually placed on the other side of the camera to the key light and close to the camera. Typically used in a **THREE-POINT LIGHTING** set-up. *See Redhead*.

FILM

   a) Celluloid strip of a certain width or **GAUGE**, from 8mm to 70mm, coated in a light-sensitive material that, when exposed to a carefully controlled light beam through the **LENS** of a camera, can record a black and white or colour **NEGATIVE** image onto the celluloid. Later, it is processed, edited and then projected at 24 frames per second. *See Editing, Neg Cutting*.

   b) A commercial film, also known as a movie, that is made to be projected in the cinema for entertainment purposes. In Europe, we tend to go and see a film. In the US, it is always a movie.

   c) Denotes use of celluloid as opposed to video.

   d) A film in television **NEWS** or in a TV magazine programme, refers to a fully edited story, **SHOT** on **LOCATION**, but on video, e.g. a studio presenter might refer to 'that film about the floods in central Europe'. This is a hangover from the fact that stories used to be shot on celluloid until video became the cheaper and quicker alternative.

FILM DIRECTOR   The person who has ultimate responsibility for what a film looks like in the cinema. From the moment of his or her appointment, the **DIRECTOR** has control of all aspects of making the film. Starts by working on the **SCRIPT** and creating a **STORYBOARD**. Works with the **CINEMATOGRAPHER** to interpret the script technically and visually. Inspires and cajoles creative excellence from the **CREW** and actors. Supervises **POST-PRODUCTION** and tries to keep within the **BUDGET** set by the **PRODUCER**. *See Director*.

FILM EDITOR

   a) Person who edits celluloid film. Works with a **FILM DIRECTOR** or **PRODUCER**, who prepares an **ASSEMBLY ORDER**. *See Editor*.

   b) Also, can refer to a video **EDITOR** who is editing **FILM** stories, working with a **REPORTER** on a television programme.

FILM EDUCATION   Alhambra House, 27–31 Charing Cross Road, London WC2H 0AU www.filmeducation.org UK charity that aims to develop the use and awareness of films, the film industry and cinema in schools and colleges. In supporting teachers, Film Education aims to give pupils the opportunity to analyse and evaluate a wide range of media. Produces a wide range of free educational materials and organises screenings, film events and workshops. Study resources include film-specific **CD-ROMs** and educational online resources, study guides, generic study guides, television programmes, study videos and new materials in **DIGITAL** video editing. Film Education sees itself as the link between the UK film industry and education, and aims to provide valuable, up-to-date film information to teachers and students. **See BFI.**

FILM PRODUCER   The person responsible for getting a **FEATURE** film made, distributed and seen in the cinema. A good **PRODUCER** has an excellent business sense, exceptional communication skills, a cool head and a sharp mind. The most important aspect of the job is finding an idea that will become a film that people will want to pay money to see. Finding the funding can be a long and exhausting process. Most films have several sources of finance. The producer must be adept at persuading people and organisations to part with their money and invest in the project. It will help investors to see the possibility of a return on their investment if the producer has enticed a major star onto the project and interested a well-known **DIRECTOR.** A viable and exciting **SCRIPT** is essential. When filming begins, the producer is responsible for how the finance raised for the film is spent. Some producers are involved with the production on a daily basis while others are less hands-on. Hiring the right **CREW**, choosing **LOCATIONS**, dealing with day-to-day problems like the weather, negotiating **CONTRACTS** for actors, dealing with agents, and keeping the whole show within **BUDGET** and on schedule, are just part of the job. During **POST-PRODUCTION**, the producer is involved with **EDITING**, distribution and publicity. Getting the film seen in a cinema can be very difficult. Over 70 per cent of British films do not get a cinema release. To be a successful film producer requires a good understanding of the technical aspects of filmmaking, razor-sharp business skills, stamina and a genuine passion for films. **See Associate Producer, Line Producer, TV Producer.**

FILM RESEARCHER   Person who looks for filmed material in **ARCHIVES**, film libraries and other sources. Searches for unusual or specific **CLIPS**. Works to a brief. Involves understanding archive pricing structures, **FORMAT** transfers and **COPYRIGHT**. Usually works in television, but can also be involved with movies.

FILM STOCK   Any film that is unexposed to light. Moving pictures for TV or movies use 35mm or 16mm film. This is the term for a roll of film before it is put in the camera and used to shoot **SCENES**. Standard roll of 16mm film that fits into a camera **MAGAZINE** is 400 feet and lasts ten minutes. Also known as raw **STOCK**.

FILTER
a) Film, photography. A filter, made of glass or **GEL**, is placed in front of the **LENS** of a camera. Used to change the way light reaches the lens, e.g. by adding colour or by **DIFFUSING** the light in a way that will create a particular 'look' to a **SCENE**. A **GRAD FILTER** can be used in a **WIDE SHOT** of countryside to make a grey sky appear blue, but not change the colour of the scenery in the lower third of the picture. There are many types of filters. Many camera operators carry a box of their favourites.
b) Sound. A sound filter is an electrical circuit that is used to take out unwanted **FREQUENCIES** from a particular sound source. These could be very high notes that might have **DISTORTED**, or the rumbling of traffic from a **NEWS** recording. **See Microphone.**

FINAL CUT PRO   Trade name for commercial professional **DIGITAL** video-editing software developed by Apple. Uses **IEEE 1394 (FIREWIRE)** to transfer data and is especially suitable for the Power Macintosh G4. The software controls the **TRANSFER** of the digital **AUDIO** and video to the computer's **HARD DISK**, where it can be edited on a **TIMELINE**. Employs a dual **SCREEN** display. One screen shows the sequence you are working on, the second, adjacent, screen shows the edited video so far. Has many **SPECIAL EFFECTS** and **FILTERS** and can be used for fully professional video editing. *See **Adobe Premiere, Avid**.*

FINE CUT   The final version of a programme or film after it has been edited. Refers to film originally, in that the fine cut includes all the **DISSOLVES** and other visual effects put in by the **EDITOR**. These are created by actually cutting the **NEGATIVE**. Also called **FINAL CUT**. *See Editing, Film Editor, Neg Cutting, Rough Cut.*

FIREWALL   Multimedia. System that prevents unauthorised access to a computer network. Typically set up by an organisation, such as a university, to protect its corporate files and those of the staff. Parts of the network may be outside the firewall and accessible to outside users with a password system.

FIREWIRE   Video editing. Trademarked name for a sophisticated cable that allows **DIGITAL** moving images to be input directly from a compatible source, such as a video camera, to a computer, for editing or storage. Also known as **IEEE 1394**. Transmits data at the fast rate of 400Mb per second. Mainly used to input the **DV** family of video recording into computer editing software. *See **Adobe Premiere, Avid**.*

FISHEYE   An extremely **WIDE-ANGLE LENS** that distorts the picture. Has the effect of looking in a convex mirror. In shooting a wide landscape, creates a wraparound effect. Used to shoot a **CLOSE-UP**, makes a face look elongated and bug-eyed. For all photography, a fisheye is the widest lens. Typically, an 8mm lens with 180-degree angle of view. Originally designed for meteorologists to photograph the clouds.

FISH POLE   SOUND. Hand-held extendable pole that holds a rifle **MICROPHONE**. Has a collapsible aluminium or carbon fibre pole about 2–2.5 metres long. The microphone is sound-insulated from the pole by a shockproof device or foam plastic. When used in an outside **LOCATION**, the microphone is covered with an artificial fur **WINDSHIELD**. The cable is taped along the pole. By holding the fish pole **OUT OF SHOT**, above a subject's head, the sound **RECORDIST** can record **DIALOGUE** without the microphone being seen by the camera. Used in television **NEWS**, **DOCUMENTARY** and drama. *See Boom.*

FLAG   Lighting. Refers to a small metal square, attached to a short pole, used to stop light **FLARE** on a set. Looks like a flag. Can be attached to a film light or positioned over the camera **LENS** to restrict light spillage.

FLARE   Lighting. Glare of light, usually from a reflective surface, on a person or on the set, that is causing a bright flash of light. Seen through the camera, this will upset the **LIGHTING CAMERAMAN** and can ruin a **TAKE**.

Flash   Multimedia. Well-known brand of software that allows the computer to read websites that have video and animated graphics. Especially important for playing computer games. *See Shockwave.*

FLASHBACK   A sequence in a film or TV programme that is outside the agreed fictional timeframe of the drama, and is a reconstruction, or visual remembrance, of past events, e.g. a quick flash of what happened to the body in a homicide case, in the film *Insomnia* (2002). *See Flashforward, Script.*

FLASHFORWARD   A sequence in a film or TV programme that is outside the agreed fictional timeframe of the drama, and is a representation, or visual suggestion, of future events. *See Flashback, Script.*

FLAT   TV. Large wall section of a TV or theatre set. Usually made of fireproofed, strong hardboard-type material that can be repainted over and over again. Some are supported by moveable struts, with weights, for a quick **STRIKE**. Can be mounted onto a low truck so that it can be wheeled into position easily. Can be fixed more securely to other flats to make room-like sets for a sitcom or drama.

FLOOD   Lighting. To adjust a **FOCUSABLE** lamp, such as a **REDHEAD**, so that it is producing an unfocused light that can light a wide area. *See Spot.*

FLOOR MANAGER   An important member of the TV studio **CREW** who is responsible for safe and efficient working on the TV **STUDIO FLOOR** – this is the entire performance area, including **AUDIENCE** seating (if appropriate) and camera movement areas. Has two-way communication with the studio **GALLERY**. Relays directions from the **STUDIO DIRECTOR** to the **PRESENTER** and **CONTRIBUTORS**, who cannot hear **TALKBACK** from the gallery. Organises studio guests, liaises with the **AFM**, has an important role in managing all the activities on the studio floor. **CUES** presenters and performers.

FLOOR PLAN   A diagrammatic map of the **TV STUDIO** floor, superimposed on a grid reference system that shows the exact positioning of the **SCENERY**, relevant large **PROPS**, studio cameras, microphone **BOOM** and other important items, as well as entrances and exits. *See Camera Script.*

FLOPPY DISK   Computer. Small square data storage device (9cm × 9.5cm) with a capacity of 1.44 **MEGABYTES**. Also known as a diskette. Useful for storing and transferring small amounts of data, as it is very portable. Too small for many software programs and has been overtaken by the **CD-ROM**, which stores about 450 times more data. *See Compression.*

FM   Radio. Frequency Modulation. System of broadcasting **SOUND** used in **VHF** radio broadcasts. Works by applying the sound signal to the **FREQUENCY** of the transmitter. The frequency of the carrier signal is **MODULATED** by the **AUDIO** signal of the programme. *See AM, Sound.*

FOCAL LENGTH   The focal length of a camera **LENS** refers to the distance from the principal point of a lens to the point at which light from a subject at infinity makes the sharpest image. It is measured in millimetres. The focal length of a standard lens on a still camera is 50mm. A **ZOOM** lens can have focal length from 80mm to 200mm.

FOCUS   An image seen through the **LENS** of a camera that is pinpoint sharp and clear is in focus. This is obtained by turning the lens so that the rays of light from the subject converge at one point. The focus is also the name for the control on the camera that adjusts the lens to create an image that is in focus. This can be done manually or automatically. *See Auto-focus.*

FOCUS PULLER   Job that involves adjusting the **FOCUS** on a film or video camera so that the subject remains in focus throughout the shot. During rehearsal for a camera move, the **LIGHTING CAMERAMAN** calls out the points at which the subject is in focus. The focus puller marks the positions on the **LENS** focus ring, with a small piece of tape. The lens has to be turned to reach the mark at the precise moment during the actual **SHOT**. The trick is in holding the focus ring in such a way that it can be rotated, without putting weight on the lens and shaking the camera or making it heavy to move. Job usually done by the **ASSISTANT CAMERAMAN**. On a movie, it is a clearly defined job in its own right.

FOG   Refers to exposed film that has been damaged by **EXPOSURE** to unwanted light. This may have been due to a fault in the camera or mishandling at the **LABS**. Creates a foggy effect that can completely cover the pictures or just obscure part of the **FRAME**.

FOLDBACK   **SOUND** played through a **SPEAKER** or headphones situated on the TV **STUDIO FLOOR**, or in a radio or sound studio. Allows the artists and audience to hear the studio sound, or sound that has been pre-recorded or originated elsewhere. Particularly useful for a singer miming to a recording, as the recording can be heard from studio speakers, but the singer can still sing into a live **MICROPHONE**.

FOLEY   Term used in the US film industry to describe creating **SOUND FX** (effects) for a movie by actually creating the **SOUNDS** required in a special sound studio, known as a Foley studio. This may mean simulating the sound of footsteps crunching on gravel, a man being punched or gunfire. The operators watch the movie action on a large screen and make the rehearsed sound effects **IN SYNC** with the on-screen actions. Named after the so-called father of movie sound effects, Jack Foley. Can be seen in action on a visit to Universal Studios in California.

FONT   Print. The size and the style of the lettering – typeface – used in a publication. Also found in word-processing software.

FOOTAGE   Film is still measured in old-fashioned feet (12 inches). For 16mm film, there are 40 frames per foot. A standard roll is 400 feet long and lasts ten minutes. Term still used to describe **SHOT** film or video material, e.g. 'how much footage have we got on the floods in the US?'

FOREGROUND   That area of the composed **SCENE** that is nearest to the camera, as seen looking through the **VIEWFINDER**.

FORMAT
   a) Print. The size and shape of the publication, e.g. A4 or A5. Also describes the way the **ARTICLES**, pictures and artwork are arranged on the page, and the binding.

b) Broadcast television. Refers to the STYLE or set-up of a programme or an individual story, e.g. quiz show format.

c) Video. Refers to the specification of the particular type of video system used, e.g. BETACAM SP, DV or DIGI BETA. There are over 20 different video formats.

fps   Frames per second. Film runs at 24 frames per second. PAL video runs at 25 frames per second. *See Frame Rate.*

FRAME

a) Film. A frame is the basic unit that makes up any film. Single rectangular picture from a roll of exposed FILM, which has a specific ASPECT RATIO. Film is projected at 24 frames per second. The size of the frame depends on the GAUGE of the film and the aspect ratio. For cinema, using 35mm or 16mm film, the standard aspect ratio is 1.33:1. Many films are made in WIDESCREEN, with an aspect ratio of 1.85:1. The Canadian IMAX projection system uses 70mm film, put through the projector horizontally, giving a huge wraparound image.

b) Video. A frame is a complete video image. PAL video runs at 25 frames per second. NTSC runs at 29.9 frames per second.

c) Camera. The frame is the rectangular outline of the area that the LENS sees, as viewed through the VIEWFINDER. Similar to the frame of a wall-hung painted picture. Can be standard TV ratio of 4:3 or widescreen, with a ratio of 16:9. *See Frame Rate.*

FRAME RATE   Video. Technical term for the number of individual FRAMES that go to make up one second of VIDEOTAPE time. Different television systems have different frame rates. NTSC has a frame rate of 29.9 frames per second. PAL is 25 frames per second. Animation companies, such as Disney, have experimented with upping the frame rate to 40 frames per second to produce smooth and fluid action sequences.

FREELANCE   Self-employed worker of any category in the media industry, who is not on the permanent staff of a company. Can be any number of roles, from REPORTER, CAMERA OPERATOR, radio or TV PRESENTER to carpenter.

FREEWARE   Multimedia. Free computer program lodged on the internet for all to use without charge. *See Shareware.*

FREEZE FRAME   A moving picture that is stopped or 'frozen' on one FRAME, in order to hold the ACTION at a certain point. Often used in sport. *See Editing, Slo-mo.*

FREQUENCY   The number of cycles an electrical signal makes in one second. Referred to as HERTZ (Hz) after the German physicist, Heinrich Hertz (1857–1894). One hertz is one cycle per second. Used to describe the electrical ANALOGUE of the pitch of a SOUND. A high sound has a high frequency. Music is made up of many frequencies.

FRESNEL LENS   Lighting. Special, heatproof, lightweight lens over a LUMINAIRE or portable lamp, which creates a steady light beam that can be FOCUSED. Pronounced 'freynell'. Invented by the Frenchman Augustine Jean Fresnel in the nineteenth century, to improve the beam in a lighthouse.

Fresnel lens on a film lamp

FROCKS   Affectionate, colloquial name for the costumes on a media production.

Frontpage   Microsoft Frontpage is industry-standard website design software. The two main software packages for creating websites are Frontpage and Dreamweaver.

F-STOP   A way of expressing the size of the APERTURE on a camera. This is the space or opening created by the IRIS. The smaller the f-stop, the larger the opening and, therefore, the more light reaches the film or CCD. On a still camera, f/1.8 might be the largest opening and f/16 the smallest. The length of time the light is allowed to come through the aperture is controlled by the SHUTTER.

FULLY PRAC   Fully practical. Refers to PROPS on a film or TV set that actually work, as opposed to being just decoration, e.g. a kettle that can be plugged into an electric circuit and produce steam and hot water on the set is fully prac.

FX   Shorthand for SOUND effects, either from a CD, DAT or created on the spot. *See Spot Sound FX.*

GAFFER   The senior electrician on a film or TV CREW. Responsible for all the electricians working under him, and for all the lighting equipment used on the set.

GAFFER GRIP   Lighting. A device used to hold a film light in an awkward position, such as above a doorway. It can be attached to the set with a suction pad or other fitting.

GAFFER TAPE   (Trade name: Gaffa) Wide, tough, sticky-backed tape with a huge variety of uses in the media industry. Especially used for taping down cables, or holding something in position temporarily.

Gaffer tape

GALLERY   The CONTROL ROOM of a TV STUDIO. Contains a VISION MIXING DESK and a bank of MONITORS. Run by the studio DIRECTOR, who has a dedicated team of professionals to put the programme on the air or record it to tape. Sits in front of the monitors, showing all the available visual sources. Works with the VISION MIXER to select and bring up the desired pictures. The **PA** calls the **SHOTS** and is responsible for timings. The technical manager is in charge of all the technical aspects of the studio. The **LIGHTING SUPERVISOR** and the **SOUND SUPERVISOR** are usually in adjacent areas. The **DIRECTOR** has full two-way communication with the **FLOOR MANAGER** and other areas such as the sound **GALLERY**.

GALLEYS   Print. Short for galley proofs. Text that has been edited and the **LAYOUT** confirmed, but has not yet been physically divided into pages. Appears as a long document rather like a roll of fax paper. *See Dummy.*

GATE   The part of a film camera or a film projector through which the film travels. In a film camera, each **FRAME** is held for a brief moment ($\frac{1}{24}$ of a second) in the gate, while the image is recorded onto the unexposed film. In a projector, the film is held momentarily so that light will shine through it and project that frame onto the screen.

GAUGE   Film. The width of a roll of film. The size of **FILM STOCK** is known by the measurement of the width of the film and the length of film. Gauge is measured in millimetres and ranges from 8mm for amateur movie-making, to 70mm, for **WIDESCREEN** films. Before video became universal in TV production, programmes shot on **LOCATION** were shot on 16mm film stock. Standard movie gauge is 35mm.

GEL   Lighting. Fireproof plastic sheeting in a variety of colours, used to cover the **LENS** of a film lamp to change the **COLOUR TEMPERATURE** of the light, e.g. the colour temperature of a standard tungsten film lamp does not match that of daylight. It has too much orange in it. To counteract this when lighting a subject with both daylight and artificial light, a **BLUE GEL** is used over the lamps to match the colour temperature of daylight. *See Filter, Lighting Cameraman.*

GENERATION   Refers to the copying of **VIDEOTAPE**. The original, or **MASTER** tape, is the first generation, and when this is copied it is a second-generation copy. A copy of a copy is third generation. Quality is affected with **ANALOGUE** tapes, but not with the copying of **DIGITAL** tapes.

GENNY   Generator. Mobile unit with a diesel or petrol motor that generates electricity. Fitted to run very quietly and usually mounted on a trailer, towed by a truck. Used to power lights and other equipment on location or to augment local power supplies.

GIF   Multimedia. Graphics Interchange Format. A file format for compressing and saving images so that they can be viewed on the internet. *See JPEG.*

GIGABYTE (Gb)   Unit of **DIGITAL** technology and measurement of data storage. A gigabyte is 1024 **MEGABYTES**.

GIGAHERTZ (GHz)   A **HERTZ** is a measurement of **FREQUENCY**. A gigahertz is one million Hz or 1000 **MEGAHERTZ**. Also used to describe the processing speed and power of a computer's chip.

GLASS SHOT   **SHOT** where the camera looks through a glass plate that has a **SCENE** or other effect painted on it, e.g. a blue sky with puffy white clouds can be painted on top of a

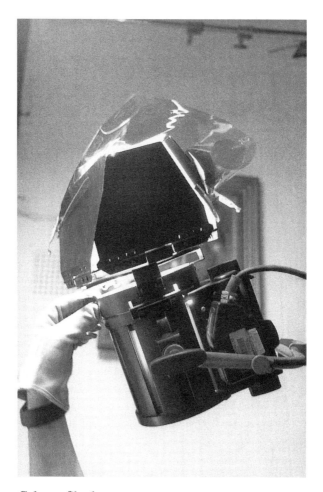

Gel on a film lamp

glass panel that is positioned between the camera and a **STUDIO** set. Actors can then appear to be delivering their lines under an attractive sky.

GNAT'S (WHISKER) Colloquial term to describe a very, very small adjustment to something. Can be a tiny adjustment to a camera move or a very fine adjustment to anything that moves in a **TV STUDIO**, on **LOCATION** or in **EDITING**, e.g. instruction to a **CAMERA OPERATOR** shooting an **INTERIOR** scene: 'Zoom in a gnat's to lose the top of the bookcase.'

GOBO Refers to any device used to deflect unwanted light from an area of a film or TV set. Colloquial for 'go between', meaning to go between a light source and the subject during the making of a film.

a) Small piece of metal used to deflect unwanted light from causing a **FLARE** on a camera **LENS**. *See Flag*.

b) Name for special form of metal pattern that can be placed like a **FILTER** in front of a film light, to create an effect or project a name, e.g. some Odeon cinemas use a light with a gobo to project their name into the entrance foyer.

c) In a **TV STUDIO**, a gobo is part of the set that allows a camera access to shoot through it, such as a window.

GO GRAMS Sound. Instruction from TV **DIRECTOR** or radio **STUDIO** director to an **AUDIO** operator to start playing a previously selected **GRAMOPHONE** record. Although records are rarely used in TV and radio production since the advent of the **CD**, this instruction can still be heard to mean 'start playing the CD'.

GPS Multimedia. Global Positioning System. System used to find an exact position on the Earth's surface. Satellites send map co-ordinates to a suitable receiver, which may be hand-held, in a car or on a yacht. Can be integrated into a phone or computer. The receiver shows geographical information on a visual display.

GRADED PRINT Film. A version of a finished and **NEG CUT** film produced by the **LABS** where the colour has been matched, but the edited film may still require colour-balancing work. It is sent back to the editor for further evaluation and colour correction so that the **SHOW PRINT** can be produced.

GRAD FILTER Graduated **FILTER**. A light filter used in photography and film that shades, from full filter at the top of the **FRAME** to clear glass at the bottom. Part is made of clear glass that gradually blends into the filter section. Used to adjust contrast or colour between a bright sky and darker landscape.

GRAIN Film. The molecular dots of silver salts in the emulsion on **FILM STOCK**. The finer the grain, i.e. the greater the number of molecules responding to light, the sharper the **QUALITY** of the image. Some filmmakers strive for a 'grainy' effect to suggest greater realism. This is associated with **DOCUMENTARY** film, shot in low light conditions, on fast film stock that accentuates the grain in the film.

GRAMOPHONE Sound. Original name for a non-electric device that plays records. Now means electric turntable with a pick-up arm that plays vinyl discs, e.g. 45 or 33⅓ rpm discs. Much favoured by DJs in clubs who use a pair of turntables to adroitly scratch and mix discs for funky 'garage' and dance beat sounds.

GRAPHICS Generic term used to describe any lettering or other artwork created for a TV show, e.g. the **TITLES** of a show often combine graphics and pictures to present the name of the show. *See Credits, Name Super, Caption*.

GRAPHICS CARD Multimedia. Device that makes it possible to read the 3D computer graphics found in computer games and on websites.

GRAPHICS DESIGNER   Creative person who designs and produces a wide variety of graphic material for a TV programme. This may be any **ON SCREEN** text such as sports scores and results, or images such as photographs. Includes integrated and animated artwork for competitions or on-screen text. Chooses the **TYPEFACE** and screen style for **NAME SUPERS** for **CONTRIBUTORS** and may organise **ROSTRUM CAMERA** work. Creates animated sequences. Works with an operator on dedicated **DIGITAL** kit to manipulate still and moving images, and combines these with **LIVE ACTION** and text to produce complex **TITLES** and **CREDITS** sequences. *See Aston*.

GREEN ROOM   In the theatre the green room is where the actors wait to go on stage. In television it is the waiting room near the **STUDIO** for programme **CONTRIBUTORS** and guests of the show.

GREEN SCREEN   Film. The film equivalent of **BLUESCREEN** or **CHROMAKEY**.

GRIP   Member of the camera **CREW** who sets up the **DOLLY** and lays **TRACK**. A more skilled job than it seems at first. The track has to be absolutely level at all points so that the camera can run smoothly, with no bumps or sideways movement. This can involve checking each section with a spirit level, and using small chocks of wood for the fine adjustments. The grip also provides the pushing power to move the camera along the track to hit the agreed end marker for each particular **SHOT**. *See Tracking Shot, Dolly In, Dolly Out*.

GROUND ROW   Floor-level lighting in a **TV STUDIO** to illuminate the base of the set or **CYCLORAMA**.

GSM   Global system for mobile communication. Mobile phone system that is widely used throughout Europe.

GUIDE TRACK   **SOUND** recorded during filming that is not for the final **SOUNDTRACK**. Usually contains **DIALOGUE**. Serves to help the **EDITOR** with **POST-SYNCHING**, where the dialogue is re-recorded in a **DUBBING THEATRE** by the actors, who deliver their lines to match the movements of their lips. *See Lip Sync*.

GUILD OF BRITISH ANIMATION   26 Noel Street, London, W1V 3RD. Represents the interests of companies involved in **ANIMATION** in the UK.

GUN MIC   Also known as a **RIFLE MIC**. Long thin unidirectional **MICROPHONE** popular with sound **RECORDISTS** because it can pick up high-**QUALITY** sound by pointing it at the sound source, e.g. a **CONTRIBUTOR** during an **INTERVIEW**. Around half a metre in length, with a coverage of about 50 degrees. Expensive popular versions, particularly by SQN, are adaptable, high-quality mics widely used in **NEWS** and **LOCATION** recording, attached to a **FISH POLE** and often encased in a furry **WINDSHIELD** to stop wind noise. The sensitive sound pick-up point is at the end of the mic. The volume and quality of the sound from the mic is checked by the sound recordist using a meter and headphones. *See Audio, Dub*.

GUNS (in production)   Using replica or real guns on a production involves hiring an **ARMOURER**. When used in a public place, requires police permission.

Gun mic

GV General view. A WIDE SHOT of a landscape, city or place that has relevance to the film or TV story. Amateur CAMERA OPERATORS tend to use a PANNING shot as a GV, but this does not allow the viewer time to take in the information. It also has the effect of trivialising an important location as somewhere that can be passed over quickly. To make the most of a GV, it needs to be carefully set up, with a good eye for artistic framing. Often several static wide shots are better at conveying a real sense of place. *See Establishing Shot.*

HANDBASHER   Hand-held battery-powered film light, often 800 watts, used to light small areas or INTERVIEWS. Often seen with NEWS camera CREWS.

HAND-HELD   Camera that is not mounted on a TRIPOD, but held in the hands or on the CAMERA OPERATOR's shoulder. Can produce shaky images associated with DOCUMENTARY programmes that may or may not be appropriate to the story. *See Steadicam.*

HARD COPY   Multimedia. Version of a computer file that has been downloaded from a computer onto paper or other printable material. *See Printer.*

HARD DISK   Multimedia. Device that stores DIGITAL data, such as computer files, and software programs on a magnetic disk system. Measured in MEGABYTES or GIGABYTES according to the amount of data it can store.

HARD DRIVE   Multimedia. Device inside the computer that physically operates a HARD DISK on the computer. A computer may have many different internal data storage areas known as hard drives.

HARD LIGHT   Lighting. Direct light from a concentrated, usually FOCUSABLE, source producing strong highlights and dark shadows. Lamps that can produce hard light include a BLONDE, a REDHEAD or an HMI. Bright sunlight is a good source of hard light that casts well-defined shadows and gives sharply defined images. Can be too bright for some situations without use of a FILTER.

HARD NEWS   Very important NEWS, of interest to everybody, often because it concerns life and death. Preferred by most EDITORS in the press and broadcasting for the opening story of any BULLETIN, e.g. the death of a president.

HARDWARE   Multimedia. The electronic equipment that makes up a computer system. This includes the MONITOR, HARD DRIVE, cables and the physical components of the computer. *See Software.*

HAZARD RISK ASSESSMENT FORM   TV, film. A form that is filled in by the PRODUCER before any filming takes place to assess the potential of the LOCATION to cause injury to anyone on the production. The form asks the producer or his nominee, to look at the potential danger areas and to assess the likelihood of any situation that may cause injury. It asks what action is being taken to minimise the potential for injury. Risks are present in all locations, e.g. filming in a boat on a lake may require trained divers in wetsuits to be present to make sure the risk of drowning or injury is minimised. Hazards are also present in a **TV STUDIO** and precautions must be taken, e.g. if a master chef is cooking on a gas hob for a cookery programme, then the correct type of fire extinguishers must be available on the set. The producer is responsible for **HEALTH & SAFETY** on a television or radio production. Risk assessment is an important part of the 1974 Health & Safety at Work Act, which states that everyone in a place of work has the responsibility for his or her own safety and for that of his or her colleagues, and even of the public if they are affected by the work going on.

HAZARD TAPE   Yellow and black tape (or other contrasting colours) that is used to alert people that they are entering a possibly dangerous area. *See Health & Safety.*

HDTV   High-Definition Television. **DIGITAL** television system that aims to equal the **QUALITY** of 35mm film. Uses 16:9 **ASPECT RATIO** and much higher **RESOLUTION**, of at least 720 progressive vertical lines and 1280 horizontal lines, roughly twice as many lines per **FRAME** as conventional TV. Growing in popularity in the US and Japan, but expensive to shoot. Needs a special HDTV receiver to benefit from the superior quality of **SOUND** and pictures. *See Aspect Ratio, Widescreen.*

HEADLINE   Broadcasting. One-sentence summary of the **NEWS** read at the beginning and/or end of a news **BULLETIN**.
   Print. Large text display at the top of a page or **ARTICLE**, attracting the reader.

HEADROOM   Looking through a camera **VIEWFINDER**, headroom is the area between the subject in the **SHOT** and the top of the **FRAME**. In an **INTERVIEW**, headroom is from the top of the **INTERVIEWEE**'s head to the top of the frame. Inexperienced **CAMERA OPERATORS** leave too much headroom. This makes the shot look wrong and makes the interviewee look weak. The head of the subject should be just below the top of the frame.

HEADSET   Device with a small **MICROPHONE** and headphone arrangement that fits over the head for two-way communication. Has many uses, e.g. the **FLOOR MANAGER** in a **TV STUDIO** can hear **TALKBACK** from the **DIRECTOR** and communicate with the **GALLERY**.

HEALTH & SAFETY   TV, radio, print, multimedia, film. Important legislation in all countries that seeks to make working conditions for employees safe and injury free. In the UK, under the 1974 Health & Safety at Work Act, everyone has responsibility for his or her own safety and for that of his or her colleagues, and even the public if they are affected by the work activity. In media productions, the **PRODUCER** is responsible at all times for the health and safety of the **CREW** and **CONTRIBUTORS**. A **HAZARD RISK ASSESSMENT FORM** is one of the most useful aids to successful safe filming with no injuries. Similar regulations exist in Europe and the US.

HELICOPTER   A video or film camera can be mounted on the front of a helicopter to take dramatic **OVERHEAD SHOTS** or **TRACKING SHOTS** that seem to defy gravity, e.g. in *Spider-Man*. A **CAMERAMAN** with nerves of steel can be strapped into a helicopter and film out of the open door to get a more varied selection of **SHOTS**. Although expensive to hire, shots from a

Helicopter used to film skiing in the Alps

helicopter are always popular with filmmakers and TV programme **DIRECTORS** for all types of programme.

HERTZ (Hz)   Electrical measurement of **FREQUENCY** of radio or **SOUND** waves. 100Hz is 100 complete cycles per second.

Hi-8   An **ANALOGUE** video-recording **FORMAT** for domestic camcorders. Now being overtaken by the superior-quality **DV** format.

HI-BAND   TV. Refers to U-matic video **FORMAT** of ¾-inch tape that was the predecessor of **BETACAM SP**.

HIGH-ANGLE SHOT   **SHOT** where the camera is placed higher up than the **EYELINE** of a **CONTRIBUTOR** or looks down on the **ACTION** from a high position, but not as high as an **OVERHEAD SHOT**.

HIGH HAT   A small, very low camera platform, used when the camera needs to be lower than the lowest setting on the **TRIPOD** or mounted on a car.

HIT   Multimedia. A way of measuring how often a website is visited on the internet. Every time someone visits a website, it gets a hit. It has become a way of assessing how successful an individual website is with the public, but it does not necessarily mean that the website is therefore a commercial success.

HMI   Lighting. A film light that produces white light of daylight COLOUR TEMPERATURE from 1200 watts going up to 18,000 watts. The name is an acronym of the symbol Hg for mercury, M for medium arc, and I for iodides, also known as a modified high-intensity discharge lamp. *See Blonde, Redhead*.

HOUSE STYLE   The particular style of visual and AUDIO production and presentation used by a media company or a television, radio or MULTIMEDIA programme. Often identified in the style of GRAPHICS used to name CONTRIBUTORS or as part of the TITLE sequence, e.g. Channel Four news has a distinctive graphics house style. A print house style might be the typeface used, the presentation of the text in terms of LAYOUT and spelling conventions, and the particular FORMAT of illustrations, page size, photographs and HEADLINES.

HOWL-ROUND   Audio. Electrical FEEDBACK from an amplified system, often heard as a continuous high-pitched SOUND from an amplifier or PA system. *See Feedback*.

HTML   Multimedia. Hyper Text Mark-up Language. Computer code used to create website pages for the internet. *See Java*.

HTTP   Multimedia. Hyper Text Transfer Protocol. Computer code that carries data from a home computer to a website. Written as http: it is part of the address of a website. This part is already in the computer's memory, so websites are known by the second part of the address, www., followed by the website name.

HUM   Audio. Low-FREQUENCY noise, usually at mains frequency of 50Hz. Can affect an audio recording or PLAYBACK. Very annoying when listening to music. Can sometimes be cured by checking and relocating earth connections on mains sockets.

HUMAN INTEREST STORY   Refers to a media story that is worthy of inclusion in a programme because of the people involved and what has happened to them, e.g. a CONTRIBUTOR may have memories of childhood that are not entirely relevant to the programme but nevertheless very interesting.

   Print. An ARTICLE that is about someone's personal experiences, e.g. the story of how a person survived a life-threatening illness.

HYPER-CARDIOID   Audio. MICROPHONE with a particularly narrow or directional pick-up pattern that is much stronger at the front and less so at the sides. Also known as a unidirectional microphone. A GUN MIC or RIFLE MIC is a hyper-CARDIOID.

HYPERLINK   Multimedia. Link to another website. An internet textual link that may be underlined and typically looks like this: www.bbc.co.uk. A webpage may contain a number of hyperlinks. When connected to the internet and clicked with the mouse, a hyperlink will take the user directly to that particular website. Typically, a hand icon will appear to notify the user that the connection will be made if clicked.

IDIOT BOARD   Large card with selected lines of script written in large letters and held just out of vision. Used by a PRESENTER or performer to help remember lines while on camera. Useful for inexperienced CONTRIBUTORS or performers with bad memories. *See Autocue.*

IEEE 1394   Firewire. Refers to a special plug on a camera and a cable, which links up with a plug on a computer that is compatible with data Fireware transfer technology. This technology allows data, i.e. pictures and sound, to be transferred to a computer from a video camera, or other accessory, at speeds of up to 400 MEGABYTES per second. Much faster than via a USB port. Especially useful for DIGITAL video EDITING, as it allows fast transfer of data into the editing software. Also known as iLink. *See Adobe Premiere, Avid, Final Cut Pro.*

IFPI   International Federation of the Phonographic Industry www.ifpi.org/home.html. The international trade association representing over 1200 record producers in over 70 countries. Useful to talk to for 'clearing' music. *See MCPS, PRS, PPL, VPL, Music Copyright, Production Music.*

iLink   *See IFEE 1394, Firewire.*

IN CUE   The first words, or first SOUNDS, of a taped TV or radio programme, e.g. in cue: FX of sea water and storm at sea ... or, in cue: I felt the rain would never stop ... The in cue appears on the CUE SHEET so that when the tape is broadcast it is clear to the broadcast technicians and the CONTINUITY ANNOUNCER where the actual story begins.

INDEPENDENT PRODUCER   Television or radio PRODUCER working on his or her own, outside a large broadcasting or production organisation. Will offer programme ideas to broadcasters, who may then COMMISSION a programme or series. The producer will then set up a production team to produce the programmes. *See Indie Production.*

INDEPENDENT TELEVISION COMMISSION (ITC)   www.itc.org.uk The Independent Television Commission (ITC). Organisation that governs and regulates commercial television in the UK. Its main concern is with maintaining standards in programming, advertising and technical areas. Also deals with complaints and can revoke broadcasters' licences. As an independent body it is funded by fees paid by its licensees. Has no power to vet programmes or interfere with scheduling, but can insist that if a programme is found to have breached its code it cannot be transmitted again in the same FORMAT. Its powers are derived from the Broadcasting Acts of 1990 and 1996. The ITC issues licences that allow commercial TV companies to broadcast in and from the UK, and regulates these services. It investigates complaints and regularly publishes its findings. It ensures a wide range of TV services are available that are of a high **QUALITY** and appeal to a range of tastes and interests. It ensures fair and effective competition in the provision of these services.

INDIE PRODUCTION   Short for independent production. Refers to a TV, radio programme or film that is made by a smaller independent company, not affiliated to the main broadcasters or the major film **STUDIOS**. There are many small, and some large, indie companies working in the broadcast arena. They tend to be able to make programmes cheaper and more flexibly than the terrestrial broadcasters. More importantly, they often come up with new and exciting ideas, especially for young audiences.

INKIE   Lighting. A small hard **FOCUS** film light of 100 watts. *See HMI, Fresnel.*

INKJET PRINTER   Computer. Printing technology that fires tiny jets of ink at the paper to create the text or photograph on the page. Domestic inkjet **PRINTERS** are very popular and have a typical **RESOLUTION** of 600×1200 **DPI**, with a print speed of between five and eight pages of text per minute, slower for pictures. Most inkjet printers use the halftone process of printing. This works by printing one of eight primary-coloured dots side by side to create different tones and shades of colour on the page. The software in the printer works out where each coloured dot should go for the best possible result. *See Scanner.*

INSERT   A short **ITEM** that is inserted into a radio or TV programme, sometimes at the last minute. An insert can be part of the planned programme, but is not as long as a sequence. *See Insert Editing.*

INSERT EDITING   Video **EDITING** where the pictures and **SOUND** must be assembled in the chosen order onto a tape that has a **CONTROL TRACK** already recorded onto it. This is the normal way to edit on **VHS**. An insert edit is where one **SHOT** or short sequence is replaced with another of exactly the same **DURATION**.

INSERT TAPE   **AUDIO** or **VIDEOTAPE** that contains some or all of the pre-recorded **ITEMS** for a programme. The items are lined up on the tape in the order of appearance in the programme, so that each one can be played in at the right place.

INSET   In a TV programme, an inset is a **FRAME** within a frame. A **GRAPHIC** or **FREEZE FRAME** of a relevant picture that is positioned via **CHROMAKEY** as an extra, smaller frame on the screen, e.g. over a newsreader's shoulder. *See Gallery.*

IN SHOT   Refers to what is in the **FRAME**. Can mean the accidental intrusion of something that should not be in the frame, e.g. the tip of a **MICROPHONE** or the **BARN DOORS** from a film light.

IN SYNC   Audio. Means the **SOUND** is perfectly aligned or synchronised with the picture on film or video. When a character speaks, the lip movements match the sound heard on the **SOUNDTRACK**. *See Out of Sync, Sync.*

INTERACTIVE   Much-used term that refers to the way a consumer of a **DIGITAL** product can influence, be involved or communicate with the **PRODUCERS** of the product. Interactivity is a benefit of the digital revolution, as it involves the internet and TV. Interactive TV provides viewers with digital TV transmission, the opportunity to communicate with a broadcaster electronically. At a basic level, this ranges from being able to buy a piece of jewellery online through a shopping channel such as QVC, or to vote for which contestant should leave the *Big Brother* house. For digital cable and satellite viewers, it is possible to select a camera from a number of different camera positions at a football match or a motor race. By pushing the interactive button on the remote control, the viewer can take part in a quiz show, see from the **POV** of a racing driver in a **LIVE** Formula 1 car, or select from a number of different endings to a drama. Future developments will increase the viewer's choice to such an extent that it may be possible to create your own TV channel by rescheduling the channels you receive. Interactivity embraces the internet by making the internet available through the TV set. This offers opportunities for the retail sector, with online banking and shopping for holidays or goods via the TV. In theory, digital interactivity offers a coming together of many communication technologies. It gives back to the consumer the power of greater flexibility in viewing, an ability to influence the broadcaster's decisions and much greater choice of entertainment and services. It is already possible to choose the time you want to watch **PAY PER VIEW** films. Interactive video games are also available. No doubt these benefits will come at a price. *See Broadband*.

INTERIOR   Any **SCENE** set inside a building or other living space. Can be an aircraft or spaceship. In a TV **SCRIPT**, written as INT and means the scene is set inside wherever the **SCRIPTWRITER** describes, as opposed to outside that area in the, possibly, fresh air. *See Exterior*.

INTERNET   Multimedia. Global network of computers linked via a **MODEM**. Can be accessed, with appropriate kit, from almost anywhere in the world. *See Hyperlink*.

INTERVIEW   An interview is a recorded conversation with someone who has agreed to take part in a radio or TV programme or be quoted in a print publication. It is a vital part of many programmes. The difference between an interview and a conversation is that the latter is not recorded or edited and has no direction. A radio interview can be conducted **LIVE** in the **STUDIO** or recorded on **LOCATION**, and edited both for time and content. A good interview needs careful preparation to get the most out of an **INTERVIEWEE**. Interviews for print and radio can be recorded on location, with a portable **MINIDISC** recorder, and edited on a computer using proprietary software such as **COOL EDIT PRO**. If an interview conducted on location is to make a significant contribution to a TV programme, it needs to be set up in a way that will look good on TV, and filmed appropriately. Interviews always look better filmed with the camera mounted on a **TRIPOD** rather than **HAND-HELD**. It's normal to have prearranged **SHOT SIZES** for a TV interview. A **CLOSE-UP (CU)**, **MEDIUM CLOSE-UP (MCU)** and **MEDIUM SHOT** or **MID-SHOT (MS)** are typical. Start with an MS and change to an MCU while a question is being asked, then go to the CU for the next question. If the interview is getting interesting or the contributor is revealing something very personal, or particularly relevant, ZOOM in vision to the CU. The DIRECTOR/interviewer must allow time while asking each question for the cameraperson to change the shot size. *See Interview Questions.*

INTERVIEWEE   Contributor to a media INTERVIEW. Person who is being interviewed for radio, TV, newspaper, magazine or the internet.

INTERVIEW QUESTIONS   The way the questions are asked in a media INTERVIEW influences the answers. The job of an interviewer is to elicit interesting, varied and perhaps revealing answers. Most interviews require research and preparation beforehand so that relevant questions can be asked. The most effective form of question is an 'open' question. This is a question that elicits more than a yes-or-no answer. Open questions are characterised by starting with the words: *who, what, when, where, why* and *how*, e.g. *How* did you escape the fire? or *What* made you take up scuba diving?

INTRANET   Multimedia. Internal network of linked computers found in a large organisation such as a university, college or company. *See Internet.*

INTRO   Short for introduction, as in the introduction to a radio or TV programme. Typically read by a studio ANCHOR or PRESENTER. Usually one or two short sentences welcoming the AUDIENCE and saying briefly what is in today's programme. Can be the short introduction to an ITEM, saying who the REPORTER is and what he or she is going to be reporting on.

i.p.s   Inches per second. Refers to the speed that AUDIO tape runs at. Generally, the faster the tape runs at, the better the sound QUALITY. Typically, speech is recorded on ¼-inch tape at 7½ i.p.s, and music at double that speed, 15 i.p.s. Magnetic ¼-inch tape used to be the most widely accepted method of recording for speech radio. Music and drama was recorded on wider MULTI-TRACK tape. However, DIGITAL recording has made the ¼-inch tape recorder redundant. *See CD+R, DAT, DV, DVD, Minidisc, Cool Edit Pro, SADiE.*

IRC   Multimedia. Internet Relay Chat. A facility that allows live conversations with other people on the internet. *See Newsgroup.*

IRIS   The iris in a camera controls the APERTURE, which is the opening through which light reaches the film, or the CCD in a video camera. Constructed of overlapping metal flaps that can be opened up to let in more light or closed down to let in less. Important component in getting the right EXPOSURE for both a photograph and a moving image. *See ASA, Shutter, Film Stock.*

ISDN   Multimedia. Integrated Services DIGITAL Network. A telecommunications line capable of carrying high-QUALITY digital data at fast speeds. Used for telephone lines, computer links and for two-way near CD-quality AUDIO.

ISP   Multimedia. Internet Service Provider. A company that provides computer users who have a MODEM with access to the internet. There are many different ISPs, e.g. AOL, ntl or Freeserve, who have permanent connections to the internet. They use very large SERVERS to route data traffic between customers and other users on the internet. *See ISDN, Broadband.*

ITC   *See Independent Television Commission (ITC).*

ITEM Radio, TV. An individual STORY – can be recorded or LIVE – in a MAGAZINE PROGRAMME. Used in both radio and TV as a way of describing any specific contribution to a programme.

JACKFIELD Audio. Rows of jack sockets that are connected to different SOUND sources, which can be 'plugged up' to form connections between sources. Commonly found in radio CONTROL ROOMS and AUDIO suites. *See BNC.*

JACK PLUG Audio. Bayonet-style electrical plug that fits into a jack socket on AUDIO and other electrical equipment. Has three connections: a positive, a negative and an earth. Larger jacks are used in SOUND studios. Mini-jack for domestic audio such as a Walkman.

Java Multimedia. Website creation software that allows websites to offer more variety and more complex services. Material that is too complex for HTML is created on Java.

JavaScript Multimedia. Programming language to create complex and interesting website design for the internet.

JIB ARM Moveable arm (up and down) that has a camera mounting at the end. A mini-jib is about two metres in length. Camera is counterbalanced with a weight and the arm pivots on a central pillar that may be mounted on a trolley. A larger, or maxi-jib, has a longer arm that could go as high as five metres, with remote controls for the camera head to control TILT and PAN. Used for TV drama or on a film. Some jib arms can be attached to a camera DOLLY to give the possibility of smooth vertical and horizontal movement in vision. A jib offers many possibilities for creative camerawork as the camera can reach into the set or provide an OVERHEAD SHOT as well as CLOSE-UP SHOTS of actors in tight situations. *See Crane.*

JIMMY JIB Form of camera CRANE with a multi-directional camera, controlled remotely from an operator at ground level through small MONITORS and joystick controls.

JOG Switchable control on the control panel of electronic kit that runs CD, DAT or video EDITING. Using the jog control, the operator can find any desired frame from a VIDEOTAPE. The jog control on an AUDIO component allows the operator to find a track or bar of music. Jog control is for very precise editing. The SHUTTLE control is for fast searching through a videotape or audio disc until the approximate point is reached. Then the jog control can pinpoint the exact frame or bar.

JPEG Multimedia. Joint Photographic Experts Group. Computer file FORMAT for pictures, with a compressed image that reduces file size for faster use.

JUMP-CUT An edit in continuous action where frames have been removed with no change of shot size, creating a 'jump' in the scene. This disturbs the smooth CONTINUITY of the scene, resulting in a jolt to the viewer. In the case of broadcast TV, or of a commercial film, this would be considered a bad edit. The **EDITOR** would be asked why there was no suitable material to replace the jump-cut. This may be the **DIRECTOR**'s fault for not shooting enough **CUTAWAYS**. A jump-cut can be done for deliberate effect, as in a Jean-Luc Godard film such as *Eloge de l'amour*. This serves to remind the viewer that the piece is a representation of reality, and not reality itself. It has been filmed and edited, and is a construct of the director and editor.

KELVIN (K)   Lighting. Degrees Kelvin is a measurement of heat, used to describe the colour temperature of light. Blue light has a high temperature and red light a low temperature.

KEY   TV. Refers to the way an electronically created MATTE or mask can be created in a TV picture, and how this matte can be replaced with another picture in an electronic keying process. The effect is to see a small picture within a larger one, or to create a WIPE or MIX. More spectacularly, this is the way CHROMAKEY, or BLUESCREEN, works when a character in a STUDIO appears to be surfing a huge wave or standing in the middle of traffic in New York. *See Virtual Studio.*

KEY LIGHT   Lighting. The main light source to illuminate a subject in a lighting set-up. In an INTERVIEW, this is the main light to illuminate the face and body. It is usually placed in front of the subject and close to the camera, but offset and slightly raised. *See Back Light, Fill Light, Three-point Lighting.*

KILOBYTE (KB)   The BYTE is a unit of DIGITAL technology. A kilobyte is 1000 bytes. *See Megabyte, Gigabyte.*

KILOHERTZ (KHz)   Unit of FREQUENCY. One kilohertz is 1000 HERTZ, or cycles per second. *See Frequency.*

KILOWATT   Lighting. Unit of electricity. One kilowatt is 1000 WATTS. Film lights are usually known by their consumption of electricity such as: 'this lamp is a 2K (2000 kilowatt) BLONDE'. *See HMI, Redhead, Three-point Lighting.*

LABS   Film laboratories where film is processed. The lab is where you send the RUSHES or DAILIES at the end of a day's filming. *See Film*.

LACE UP   To thread film through the GATE and transport mechanism of a film camera or PROJECTOR.

LANDSCAPE   Print. Describes a page set-up that is rectangular, but wider (longer horizontally) than it is high, usually in a ratio of about 4:3. *See Portrait*.

Landscape page set-up

LANYARD MICROPHONE   MICROPHONE that is worn around the neck or under a tie. Also called a LAVALIER. *See Microphone*.

LAVALIER MICROPHONE   *See Lanyard Microphone*.

LAYOUT   Print. Draft drawing of how a page design of a MAGAZINE or book might look. Can be quite detailed, showing size, colour and FONT of the text and where it will be placed on the page, in relation to relevant design details or artwork, or may be just a sketch that a designer will work on. *See Dummy, Galleys.*

LCD   Liquid Crystal Display. A flat screen displaying colour pictures, typically found on a modern DIGITAL camera, laptop computer and on some camcorders. Pulls out from the camera like opening a small book and acts as an extra VIEWFINDER. Can be difficult to see in bright sunlight. Also useful for viewing previously recorded sequences. Many other pieces of equipment use an LCD screen, e.g. a digital clock.

LEADER

a) Film. Special length of celluloid printed with in-vision numbers, counting down from ten, spliced onto the beginning of a film or film story. It leads into the film itself. There is also a sound leader for SEPMAG films.

b) TV. Video leader is a standard video sequence at the start of all programmes, giving details of the programme, with an in-vision countdown of up to 30 seconds.

c) Radio. Programmes made on ¼-inch tape have a length of yellow, non-magnetic tape at the beginning, known as a leader. The leader is wound round the take-up spool to the point where it is spliced onto the magnetic tape with the programme on, and so the actual programme can be lined up to start right at the beginning.

LEAD STORY   The main story that starts a TV or radio NEWS bulletin or current affairs programme.

Print. The main story, usually in big headlines on the front page of a newspaper, or the important first feature ARTICLE in a publication. *See Copy, Feature.*

LEGS   Colloquial term for a camera TRIPOD.

LENS   Expertly crafted glass instrument, designed to concentrate and FOCUS light onto a FRAME of celluloid film or onto the PIXELS in a video or DIGITAL camera. Used on still and moving-image cameras. There are many types of lenses with a variety of FOCAL LENGTHS. One of the widest is an 8mm FISHEYE lens, giving a distorted but panoramic view of a SCENE. A 1200mm lens is one of the narrowest, with an angle of view of two degrees. The QUALITY of the lens, and the way it is manufactured, contribute to the overall image quality. The selection of the right lens for the circumstances is one of the most important and crucial creative decisions for a LIGHTING CAMERAMAN or photographer.

LETTERBOX   FORMAT for showing films on a standard television set. The film is shown with the top and bottom of the screen masked off, to create a letterbox effect, allowing the film to be shown in its original ASPECT RATIO. Most domestic televisions are 1.33 times as wide as they are high, that is, they have an aspect ratio of 4:3. To show films on TV, most have about 45 per cent of the visual area removed from the screen in a process called 'pan and scan'. This concentrates on one section of the picture, usually where the most important action is taking place, and fills the conventional screen with this section. The advantage of a WIDESCREEN television is that this is not necessary. The letterbox process takes the entire FRAME and reduces the size in proportion so that it fits within the width of the TV. This allows the film to be seen in its original aspect ratio, as the filmmakers intended it to be. The black areas at the top and bottom of the screen are unused parts of the screen, but can be useful for putting in SUBTITLES. *See Anamorphic Lens.*

LIBEL   A simple definition of the legal term, libel is telling lies about someone. To commit libel, a broadcaster or publication would have to broadcast or print something that was an unfair and unreasonable defamation of a person's character. The courts normally apply the following criteria to test if a statement is defamatory: does it expose a person to hatred, ridicule and contempt, or cause him or her to be shunned and avoided? Does it injure the person's livelihood? Does it reduce a person in the eyes of right-thinking people? Libel can happen by implication. A TV news clip showing a man being arrested could imply that he has committed a criminal act. The man could sue for libel if it turned out that he was innocent. The COMMENTARY needs to make it clear that he is not a criminal until proved so in a court of law. Someone can claim that a defamatory statement has been about them if that person can be identified, e.g. a broadcast item may say that all plumbers in a certain small town are useless. If there were three of them, then each one could say they had been defamed. It is definitely not safe to assume that because something has been written in a newspaper then it can be repeated on radio or TV, e.g. a TABLOID paper accuses a famous footballer of stealing a Ferrari. If this is reported on a NEWS bulletin and is subsequently found to be false, the footballer could sue both the broadcaster and the tabloid for defamation. There are three principal defences that a journalist or broadcaster could use against libel, but it can be difficult to convince a sceptical jury:

a) justification – can the journalist prove, with reliable evidence, that the statements are the truth;

b) fair comment – was the statement a fair and honest comment of public interest and based on fact; the journalist has to prove that the opinion is honestly held and based on fact;

c) privilege – can the statement in a broadcast or publication be taken from fair and accurate reports of court proceedings, parliamentary proceedings or public meetings.

Libel laws are tougher in the UK than in the US or Europe, and large damages have been awarded against newspapers and broadcasters. It pays to check all copy against the possibility of libel.

LIBRARY FOOTAGE   VIDEOTAPE or film from a film library that is used in a programme. *See Archive, Clips, Stock Footage.*

LIGHTING CAMERAMAN   The leading male or female cameraperson in a film or TV CREW, who is responsible for the picture composition, the framing and the lighting for each SHOT. An experienced and knowledgeable camera operator will seek to interpret the DIRECTOR's vision and provide the finest-QUALITY pictures. Influences the look and style of a film. Knows how to light any SCENE. Can recreate the look of a period with lighting as in Sam Mendes' Oscar-winning *Road to Perdition*. Responsible for the GRIP, ASSISTANT CAMERAMAN, FOCUS PULLER and GAFFER, and for the electricians who set up and adjust the lighting. Selects the correct EXPOSURE, sets FOCUS and chooses the most suitable LENS for the shot. On a big shoot, the camera is operated by a CAMERA OPERATOR. *See Cinematographer*.

LIGHTING GELS　Translucent plastic sheeting that has been accurately coloured to change the light temperature of the light coming from a film lamp. Fitted over the front of the lamp or the BARN DOORS with special clamps. *See Gel, Colour Temperature*.

LIGHTING PLAN　A specially drawn diagram of a TV or film STUDIO, showing the precise location of each lamp, indicating which ones and what type are to be used for a particular production. Drawn up by the LIGHTING SUPERVISOR.

LIGHTING RIG　The metal structure that is suspended from the ceiling of a TV STUDIO to hold the large number of lamps required for a TV show or film. At rock concerts, OBs and film sets, the lighting rig refers to the whole vast lighting set-up and support system.

LIGHTING SUPERVISOR　The senior lighting technician, in charge of all lighting in a TV studio or on an OB.

LIGHTWORKS　Trade name for one of the first high-QUALITY professional computer-based OFFLINE digital video-editing systems. Characterised by a user-friendly hand-control system based on the one used by film editors on a STEENBECK film-editing table. *See Avid*.

LINEAR EDITING　Video EDITING where the pictures and sound are edited together in the correct order. To change the order of some of the material, the edit has to be started all over again. It is possible to insert small sections as long as a piece of the same DURATION is taken out. When programmes were first made on video, this was the only method of editing. Since the advent of DIGITAL editing, virtually all television and radio programmes are edited, at least initially, by a NON-LINEAR system.

LINE PRODUCER　The PRODUCER's deputy on a TV drama shoot or film. Manages and is responsible for the routine day-to-day activities of filming, including rejigging SCHEDULES, overseeing the BUDGET and dealing with the many problems that can happen during a shoot. Needs to be level-headed, tactful, diplomatic, and good at organisation and planning ahead. *See Associate Producer, Film Producer, TV Producer*.

LINE-UP
a) Time set aside before recording begins in a TV STUDIO day, to adjust and set up the TV cameras so that they all produce compatible pictures.
b) A professional video camera is lined up using COLOUR BARS to produce standardised pictures. A professional camcorder will generate its own colour bars that will be recorded and used to line up the pictures it produces during the ONLINE EDIT.

LINE-UP TONE　Sound. An AUDIO signal at 1000Hz, sent at zero level to an audio mixer or other audio equipment, as a mean standard for setting up sound levels common to all equipment. *See Hertz*.

LINKS　Radio. The words spoken by the PRESENTER or NARRATOR, linking together recorded material such as INTERVIEWS in a factual radio programme.

LIP MIC   Sound. MICROPHONE in a special holder that allows the user to speak very closely into the sensitive area. The aim is to severely restrict unwanted noise, such as crowd noise at a football match. Most common use is as a COMMENTATOR's mic.

LIP SYNC   The synchronisation (SYNC) of an actor's lip movements with the DIALOGUE he or she is speaking. When the lip movements and the SOUND are not synchronised, the SCENE is OUT OF SYNC. Sometimes it is necessary to shoot part of a scene so that the actors' lip sync cannot be seen. This offers opportunities for cutting dialogue or speeding up the ACTION in EDITING.

LIVE   Broadcast on radio or TV of a programme, event or activity as it actually happens, e.g. a football match or a breakfast show. Most daytime radio TRANSMISSIONS are live as they are taking place at the time the listener hears them, although some items may be recorded. A broadcast live event on television and radio that does not take place in a STUDIO is known as an OB (Outside Broadcast). TV uses a MULTI-CAMERA set-up and a SCANNER vehicle to record the pictures and SOUND or relay them via a satellite or cable link to the broadcaster. Live programmes, such as NEWS BULLETINS, are broadcast every day from broadcasters' studios.

LIVE ACTION   Term used to distinguish moving-image action by living people or animals from animated sequences. A GRAPHICS DESIGNER creating a TITLE sequence for a FACTUAL PROGRAMME may integrate live action SHOTS of some of the people taking part in the programme with animated GRAPHICS. *See Animation, CGA, CGI.*

LIVE LINK   PRESENTER or REPORTER broadcasting LIVE. This may be from a different LOCATION to the studio ANCHOR, e.g. a live link from a NEWS reporter in Washington.

LOCATION   The place where the shoot, filming, broadcast, recording or even rehearsal takes place that is not in a STUDIO. Being on location can be anywhere away from the production office. Usually, a location is selected as it is relevant to the SCRIPT and adds to the authenticity of sequences SHOT there. Many locations are transformed by the art director, with judicious set-dressing, especially for period productions, where houses may be repainted and shop-fronts disguised with period features. Choosing a suitable filming location is often done by a LOCATION MANAGER. There are a number of things to look out for. Permission for using the location is required and a RELEASE FORM is signed. The direction of the sun as it moves over the site during the day can dictate where the filming takes place, and there must be no nearby sources of extraneous noise, e.g. a motorway. For a film or major drama, there will be a number of trailers – small mobile homes – for actors and CREW. Parking will need to be found for them, the chuck wagon (mobile restaurant), the honey wagon (mobile lavatory), as well as generators *(see Genny)* and equipment vans. Some locations, such as a semi-detached house, may be small and the support vehicles will be parked elsewhere. The location manager has to be aware of many things when searching for a suitable location – not least how much it may cost. A stately home as a major feature film location, such as the one featured in the Robert Altman film *Gosford Park*, would charge upwards of £1500 per day.

LOCATION CATERING   Food provided by specialist catering companies at the filming LOCATION. Known as the chuck wagon, high-quality hot and cold food and drink is provided for notoriously hungry CREW and cast. Can be a big operation with marquees for a major movie. Often it is one or two vehicles that act as kitchen and small dining room, offering good food and shelter from the elements. It is nearly always cost-efficient to provide on-site catering for production staff and actors, close to the set. This allows for regular breaks and provides catering at the unsociable hours when filming often takes place, such as during the night or very early in the morning.

LOCATION MANAGER   Member of the TV or film production team who is primarily responsible for researching, finding and setting up suitable INTERIOR and EXTERIOR LOCATIONS for a shoot. Large broadcasting and film companies have data banks of recommended locations, but all locations have to be RECCED. The film may require a street to be cordoned off for an early morning shoot. The location manager would have to get police permission for this and any use of mock firearms in a public place (*see Guns*). Security services would have to be engaged to ensure no onlookers disrupt the shoot. For period dramas, a large park and stately home may be required, which could be very costly. May have many other responsibilities, including managing the BUDGET, organising SCHEDULES, checking SAFETY procedures, booking accommodation, acquiring kit, arranging transport and altering the location to suit the art director's wishes.

LOCKED OFF   Refers to locking a camera in a certain position so that it does not move at all. This offers possibilities for a number of popular visual effects that can be achieved in POST-PRODUCTION, such as time-lapse sequences, e.g. where an empty railway station suddenly fills with people in a few screen seconds. The camera has been locked off in one position and on one SHOT SIZE. This ensures that the static objects in the FRAME, such as the buildings, do not move when the film or video is played back faster than normal. The people, however appear and disappear in speeded-up mode giving a visual diary of the events of many hours in a few seconds. The same technique is used to film clouds, dramatically moving at speed across the sky. Where the camera wants to capture the change of seasons or other long-term effect, a locked-off camera position can be set up and carefully marked. The camera can be taken away and returned to exactly the same position to take a sequence of locked-off shots over a long period. *See Crane, Pedestal, Tripod.*

LOGO   Company motif or symbol, designed to create a memorable image that the public can remember and associate with a product, programme, TV channel or broadcaster, e.g. the distinctive channel logos for Sky TV and Channel 4, the Nike swoosh logo.

LOG SHEET   Record of all the relevant information pertaining to a SCENE or sequence taken on the set during filming. Normally kept by the PA. Includes the DURATION of each TAKE, SHOT SIZE, details of costume or any special PROPS, and a record of the characters in the scene. May include notes on what went wrong on a bad take or whether there was a false start. Often includes an indication if a particular take is the one the DIRECTOR would like to use at the edit. May include a variety of notes to do with the LOCATION, weather, time of day or technical issues that could be useful to the director and FILM EDITOR in POST-

PRODUCTION. After shooting on a drama, the PA will reproduce the notes onto a copy of the SCRIPT. This MARKED-UP script will be invaluable to the EDITOR as work starts on editing the show.

LONG SHOT (LS)   A SHOT of a person that includes the full length of the subject, from head to toe. Taken from some distance away and including some of the setting and background. *See Shot Size, Very Long Shot (VLS).*

Long shot

LOW-ANGLE SHOT   For a low-angle SHOT, the camera is placed well below the subject's EYELINE and looks up at the subject. It can placed at floor level or below to get a shot of a rock singer on a stage or a speaker at a meeting. Often, this angle gives the impression of power and importance to the subject. *See Shot Size.*

LUMINAIRE   Lighting. General term for a dedicated film or TV light. Often used to describe the large lights found in TV STUDIOS. *See Fresnel Lens, Lighting Rig.*

LUMINANCE   Video. The observation of luminance is brightness. Luminance is the name for the brightness part of a video signal.

MAGAZINE   Film. The lightproof cover that holds the roll of raw **STOCK** and clips into a film camera. It feeds the unexposed film into the camera and then winds the exposed film back onto another spool within the **MAGAZINE**. This is taken out and put in a **FILM CAN** to be taken to the **LABS** for processing. The **CAMERA** assistant loads a new roll of film into each of several magazines before and during shooting, so there is always one ready for the camera. A roll of film for a 16mm camera is normally 400 feet and lasts ten minutes.

Print. A regularly produced publication containing a variety of **ARTICLES**, usually with theme-based content, such as celebrities or automobiles.

MAGAZINE PROGRAMME   A programme for TV or radio that is made up of a number of different **ITEMS** and stories on a variety of subjects. A universal part of any talk radio **SCHEDULE**, such as BBC Radio 4, e.g. *Woman's Hour* or *You and Yours*. Television magazine programmes tend to come under a category such as travel, breakfast shows or business.

MAKE-UP ARTIST   Creative person who supervises and administers cosmetic make-up, hairstyles, wigs and other effects required to prepare actors for camera. Make-up artists have a comprehensive knowledge of hairstyles and facial appearances of people through the ages, according to the fashions of the time, as well as an understanding of how facial texture and skin colour can be made to look natural on camera.

M & E   Music and Effects (FX). Name for a moving-image **SOUNDTRACK** that includes all the music and all the **SOUND FX** for a moving-image production. These have been mixed to create one M & E **TRACK**. This track can be mixed with the **DIALOGUE** or speech content of the programme at the **DUB**, to create the final **MIX**. Feature films and broadcast programmes often have a separate M & E track so that dialogue can be added as an additional track in any language, or for **DVDs** in several languages. *See Track Lay.*

MARGIN   Print. Space left at the sides of a **COLUMN** on a page of a publication.

MARKETING   All media products need selling to an **AUDIENCE**. Marketing is the whole ensemble of strategies used to sell a film, TV programme or any other media product. Marketing research identifies needs and trends, and influences the way products are advertised. Increasingly, the internet is an important marketing tool, used to great effect by the film, *The Blair Witch Project*. Traditional methods of advertising are also very important in selling a media product to a mass global audience, e.g. **PRESS RELEASE**, poster, giant hoarding, film or TV **TRAILER**, newspapers, **MAGAZINES** and radio. Press comment, first-night parties and product placement all contribute to the marketing campaign of a feature film or TV series.

MARK IT On a film set you will hear the CAMERA OPERATOR signify that the camera is rolling and the SCENE is ready to be recorded, by giving the instruction to 'mark it'. An assistant will show the CLAPPERBOARD to the camera, to provide a visual marker of the scene number and other information. If there is SYNC SOUND, the arm on the clapperboard is snapped down to make the distinctive sharp clap that will enable the editor to SYNC up the pictures with the SOUND. *See End Board.*

MARK-UP Refers to the way a TV STUDIO director will annotate his or her SCRIPT for a LIVE show or TV recording. This involves marking notes in pencil on the script, adding extra directions or reminders, and making the script easier to read while looking at the MONITORS. Also refers to the POST-PRODUCTION script for a drama that is marked up by the PA, with details of each take for each scene. *See Log Sheet.*

MASTER SOUND recording. Produced from the MULTI-TRACK recording made in the recording STUDIO, the final twin-track stereo mix is known as the master. This is the one from which the commercial CD is made.

MASTER SHOT A WIDE SHOT used in a drama production that covers the main action in a particular SCENE or sequence. Movies and major TV dramas record the DIALOGUE material using just one camera. (A major ACTION set-up, such as a war scene involving expensive explosions, would be recorded on several cameras.) DIRECTORS and actors prefer to work by setting up and lighting one scene at a time. The master shot is recorded first. The action is then repeated while each CLOSE-UP shot is recorded.

MATTE

a) Film. A matte is a mask that covers some of the FRAME so that only part of the film will be exposed. Another SHOT can be added later by exposing the area covered by the matte to make a composite shot. Used in early films to create SPECIAL EFFECTS. Modern techniques rely more on computer effects. *See CGI.*

b) TV. A matte is a cut-out of an image, such as a keyhole, through which a camera can shoot another scene, creating a 'through the keyhole' effect. Also, a matte can be used as an electronic KEY for other images. *See Chromakey.*

MATTEBOX A specially designed attachment for holding a MATTE or FILTER that fits in front of the LENS of a camera.

MCPS Mechanical Copyright Protection Society Tel: 020 7306 4500 Fax: 020 7306 4380 www.mcps.co.uk The music rights society in the UK that protects COPYRIGHT and collects ROYALTIES on behalf of songwriters, composers and music publishers. Collects royalties any time copyrighted music is copied, e.g. to make a promotional video, a music CD or for broadcasting. The MCPS licenses PRODUCTION MUSIC and can supply a full list of over 60 specialist libraries. *See PPL, PRS.*

MCU *See Medium Close-Up (MCU).*

MEDIA PLAYER Computer. Software that plays downloaded or streaming AUDIO, e.g. a DIGITAL radio station on a computer. Popular examples include the trade names Windows Media Player, Realplayer and Quicktime.

MEDIAWATCH-UK www.mediawatchuk.org Formerly The National Viewers and Listeners Association, originally set up by Mary Whitehouse. UK organisation concerned with standards of taste and decency in broadcasting, video and film. Keeps pressure on the broadcasting authorities to improve their public accountability and to explain their policies on taste and decency in the media. Involved in 1984 campaign to outlaw 'video nasties'. A Private Members' Bill was introduced in Parliament requiring videos to be classified by age suitability, in a similar way to films shown at the cinema. Involved in the campaign for the Protection of Children Act in 1978 that effectively made child pornography illegal. This Act enables police action to be taken against those who use the internet to publish and make available indecent images of children. *See Voice of the Listener & Viewer (VLV)*.

MEDIUM CLOSE-UP (MCU) Slightly wider than a CLOSE-UP. A head-and-shoulders SHOT that is the usual size for a television INTERVIEW, with the bottom of the frame just along the line of the top pocket of a man's jacket, hence its name top-pocket shot. *See Shot Size.*

Medium Close-Up (MCU) shot

MEDIUM LONG SHOT (MLS) Wider than a MEDIUM SHOT (MS) but not as wide as a LONG SHOT. For a subject that is standing up, the bottom of the frame in the VIEWFINDER should be no lower than the knees of the person. *See Shot Size.*

Medium Long Shot (MLS)

MEDIUM SHOT (MS)   Shot of a person that is wider than a MEDIUM CLOSE-UP (MCU). The bottom of the frame in the VIEWFINDER cuts off at the waist, whether the person is sitting down or standing up. Standard shot of a television PRESENTER in the STUDIO, showing the top half of the person. *See Shot Size.*

MEGABYTE (Mb)   The main unit of digital technology is the BYTE. A megabyte equals 1,048,576 bytes. *See Kilobyte (Kb).*

MEGAHERTZ (MHz)   A HERTZ is a measurement of FREQUENCY. A megahertz is 1000Hz. Also used as the measurement of a computer chip's processing speed and power. *See Gigahertz.*

MERCHANDISING   Consumer materials and goods associated with a media product, such as a film or TV series. A large variety of goods are put on sale displaying a COPYRIGHTED logo or image, and will generate extra income for the original product. It is both a way of developing public awareness and providing a source of finance for small and large projects. Key aspects of successful merchandising are creating a winning image and locating the most effective point of sale. Also, setting up a website that promotes the product and sells the merchandise. Merchandising can greatly increase the income of a successful film, as in the case of *Harry Potter and the Chamber of Secrets*. A range of attractive merchandise will undoubtedly enhance the profile of the film, MULTIMEDIA product or TV series and make money. Well-known merchandising outlets include Disney shops, selling items imprinted with logos and images owned by Disney, such as Winnie-the-Pooh.

MICROPHONE (MIC)   Converts acoustic SOUND waves into electrical signals that can be stored on tape, disc or computer. There are a large variety of microphones in use in radio, AUDIO work, film and TV. Microphones are categorised in several main ways. According to their directional sound pick-up pattern, the job they do, and their type. A microphone can be OMNIDIRECTIONAL, which means it is sensitive to sound in a 360-degree pattern around the mic, with nearly equal sensitivity in all directions. A UNIDIRECTIONAL mic picks up sound only from the sensitive end, and so cuts out a lot of background noise. A bidirectional mic picks up sound, typically, from two opposing sides. One of the most useful for radio interviews and general purposes is the CARDIOID mic, which picks up sound in a heart-shaped pattern – about 160 degrees – around the sensitive area. This makes it ideal to hold between two people for an INTERVIEW. Mics are also categorised by type, as follows.

a) Personal, lapel, LANYARD, LAVALIER or neck. Small clip-on mic that can be attached to a shirt, lapel or collar or hidden under a necktie. Often used for a TV studio interview, as it has a cable attached to a sound socket located in the STUDIO wall. Can be used on LOCATION, with the cable attached to a portable SOUND MIXER or directly to the camera.

Microphones at a live music recording

b) Radio. Similar to a personal mic, but attached to a radio transmitter that is carried in the back pocket or on a belt. The sound **TRANSMISSIONS** are picked up by a receiver attached to a field camera or to the sound **RECORDIST'**s portable **MIXER**. Useful on location and for a **PRESENTER** moving around.

c) Rifle or gun. All-purpose unidirectional mic, shaped like a rifle. As the name suggests, you point the barrel of the mic towards the sound source. Has a very narrow pick-up pattern. Very good for general work on location. Commonly seen at press conferences with a furry **WINDSHIELD** at the end of a **FISH POLE**.

d) Stick or hand-held. Robust, stick-like and often rather chunky mic, either with a cable attached or with a built-in radio transmitter, favoured by TV presenters interviewing members of the public.
See Fish Pole, Boom, Sound.

MIDI   Musical Instrument Digital Interface. Computer language that is used to communicate data directly between musical instruments and a computer. Describes music using a fixed set of parameters. Its pitch, volume and the start and end time describe a note. Most instruments, such as guitars, keyboards and drums can be configured into a midi format. The midi signal is used to identify and activate sounds that are already stored as digital samples or created with a synthesiser. The midi computer code can be recorded and manipulated using a computer sequencing programme, so the music can be edited in a number of ways, such as making it go faster or slower, shorter or longer.

MID-SHOT (MS)   Shows the top half of a person, from the waist to the top of the head, leaving a small amount of **HEADROOM**. *See Medium Shot, Shot Size.*

MINIDISC   **SOUND**-recording digital **FORMAT** developed by Sony, using a disc that looks like a small version of a PC floppy disk. The music format is known as Atrac – Adaptive Transform Acoustic Coding – and has **CD** quality. Can record up to 70 minutes of high-**QUALITY** sound on a standard disc. Some recorders have a reduced-quality longplay option. Used extensively for radio **INTERVIEWS** and **LOCATION** sound recording. Minidiscs with pre-recorded commercial music were available, but were not considered a success. *See DAT.*

MINS   Minutes. Used in a radio or TV **SCRIPT** to denote **DURATION**, e.g. two mins. Also written 2'. See **SECS**, e.g. 4 mins and 30 secs can be written 4' 30''.

MISE-EN-SCÈNE   Originally, a French term that means 'put in the scene'. It has come to mean everything that the **DIRECTOR** and the production team have selected to be included in the **FRAME** to give meaning to a **SCENE**. This includes the design of the set, costume, make-up, **PROPS** and the positioning of the actors. It can also include the way the scene is shot. The choice of **CAMERA ANGLES** and **LENS**, use of **FILTERS** and **SOUND** design, and the lighting.

MIX

a) TV, film. Gradual transition from one image to another. Achieved either in electronic editing, on film or in the **GALLERY** of a **TV STUDIO**. *See Dissolve, Wipe.*

b) Sound. Transition from one sound source to another through a **SOUND MIXING DESK**. Can be slow and include a **FADE**, or quick.

c) Another name for the sound **DUB**, where soundtracks are mixed together to create a final **MIX**.

MIXER   Audio. Equipment used to combine different **SOUND** sources, such as studio **MICROPHONES** and music on **CD**. A radio studio mixer typically has 24 channels (sound sources) or more. A location sound **RECORDIST** will use a portable mixer, which may have four or more channels, to mix several microphone inputs. *See Sound Mixing Desk.*

MODEM   Multimedia. Device that connects the computer to the internet via a telephone line and/or a **BROADBAND** connection. A standard telephone modem has a maximum speed of 56Kbps.

MODULATION   Radio. The process of impressing **AUDIO** and/or video information onto a carrier signal to transmit radio signals. If it is varied in amplitude, it is called **AM** or Amplitude Modulation. If it is varied in **FREQUENCY**, it is known as **FM** or Frequency Modulation, also called **VHF**.

MONITOR   High-quality, colour or black-and-white television set, used to view or monitor **VISION** only. Monitors are found wherever the technical **QUALITY** of the moving image is important, such as a TV studio **GALLERY**, to view the output of cameras and other visual sources. A high-quality colour monitor is used to view the studio **OUTPUT** or final picture that will be transmitted or recorded. Also used on **LOCATION** to view the output of a film or video camera. Does not usually have a built-in broadcast TV receiver or a loudspeaker.

MONTAGE   A sequence of short images, stylishly edited together to act as visual punctuation in a **DOCUMENTARY** or for a particular effect in a feature film. Comes from the French word 'monter', meaning to mount, set or put together something, like a jewel. Often, the images are edited to a music **SOUNDTRACK**.

MORAL RIGHTS   The moral rights code is part of the 1988 **COPYRIGHT** Act and deals mainly with the rights of authors and scriptwriters, and the rights of privacy over certain materials. Moral rights are additional rights, granted only to the author of copyright literary, dramatic, musical or artistic work, and to the director of a copyright film. One of the main moral rights is the right to be identified as the author of a work and have your name credited in public as such. This right has to be asserted and does not happen automatically. Also, the right to privacy of certain photographs and films that can result in the stopping of publication of private archives. These rights can lead to lengthy court cases, especially in Hollywood.

MORPH   TV, film. The process of in-vision transformation of a person or object into another person or object. In the film *Harry Potter and the Philosopher's Stone*, a black cat transforms in vision into the teacher played by Maggie Smith. Morphing is particularly used to show a character's face becoming older or younger, or to transform someone or something into something completely different. This is done particularly effectively in the BBC information campaign to publicise the new free-to-air TV service, called '*Freeview* the new face of television'. Here, well-known TV characters appear to peel off their own faces to reveal those of other well-known people.

MOVIE CAPTURE   Multimedia. Software that allows a computer to DIGITISE, record and store moving images. Used in video EDITING systems, such as ADOBE PREMIERE and FINAL CUT PRO. *See Avid, Batch Digitising, Firewire.*

MP3   Computer. Way of storing SOUND in DIGITAL FORMAT. Computer file format for digital music that can be distributed over the internet. MP3 software is needed to play back these files at near-CD quality.

MU   Musicians Union. The main union in the UK for all working musicians.

MULTI-CAMERA PRODUCTION   A video recording, or OB, where more than one interlinked camera is used. Cameras are linked via cables or radio links to a SCANNER vehicle, which has full video and SOUND mixing facilities and high-QUALITY video recording. Used for televising large events such as the Olympics, football matches and horse-racing. *See Live.*

MULTI-LAYERING   Combining two or more DIGITAL picture sources in a video or photo edit to produce a composite final image. *See CGI.*

MULTIMEDIA   The merging of DIGITAL skills and FORMATS to create digital media, such as website design and production. A website can include not only TEXT, but also GRAPHICS, moving images, flashing commercial messages, interactive systems for message boards and NEWSGROUPS, as well as the ability to translate ideas into the computer language of website design.

MULTIPLEX   Multimedia. A UHF frequency that can transmit several channels and data services in the space of one ANALOGUE TV channel. Currently, as many as seven channels, with several DIGITAL text and radio services, can be fitted onto one multiplex. Part of the digital revolution, as it allows many digital radio stations to broadcast on one frequency, saving money and bandwidth. Also the generic name for your local multi-cinema complex, but this is not technical.

MULTI-TRACK RECORDING   SOUND recording technique where many sound sources are recorded onto one tape as separate TRACKS. Large recording tapes can hold up to 128 tracks. The main tape deck in a sound recording STUDIO is known as a multitrack, and records from a large SOUND MIXING DESK. This means that in recording a rock band or symphony orchestra, each instrument can have its own sound source, e.g. lead guitar is recorded onto one track. If there is a mistake in the guitar solo, just this section can be recorded again. The best tracks are selected and mixed together to make the two tracks of the stereo MASTER tape. *See Dub, Mix, Sound Mixing Desk.*

MUSIC (in productions)   Nearly all productions for film or TV have music as part of the SOUNDTRACK. Music is normally specially composed or arranged for a feature film, and for some TV productions. There are always COPYRIGHT considerations to be taken into account when copying music or using music for any commercial project. Commercial CDs have to be specially cleared to be played on broadcast TV. Major broadcasters, such as the BBC, have comprehensive copyright agreements with the recording companies and copyright collection agencies such as the MCPS, PRS, PPL and VPL. However, this does not mean that every commercial CD can be used on any programme. Some bands and record labels will not give permission under any circumstances – the Rolling Stones are noted for rarely allowing their recordings to be used out of context. *See Production Music.*

MUSIC COPYRIGHT   Complex area but worth getting your head round. Any broadcast or other professional use of published music is covered by COPYRIGHT and there will be ROYALTIES payable for broadcast use. For a music CD, the following typically have rights: artist, composer, lyric writer, producer, arranger, record label and publisher. These details can be found on a CD insert card or on the label. All commercial recordings must be 'cleared' for broadcasting or for use in a video that is going to be sold to the public. There are two basic rights that must not be infringed: the rights to the music work itself, e.g. John Lennon's '*Imagine*' exists as words and music, and as a sound recording. Both sets of rights have to be cleared for broadcast and paid for. The rights to the musical work itself, known as 'the song', are obtained from the MCPS or the copyright owner. The rights to the mechanical copying of the sound recording are most often obtained from the record company or from one of the copyright societies – PPL, VPL or BPI. To use a recording, the record company must give permission for the disc to be copied for broadcast – going out LIVE counts as copying – and other rights holders may have to be asked. Fortunately, in most cases commercial CDs can be cleared through music rights societies, such as the MCPS and PPL, who collect royalties on behalf of the owners. Large broadcasters, such as the BBC and Sky, will have blanket licence agreements with the main societies for most broadcasting purposes, but this does not cover all labels and all commercial recordings. If in doubt, check before broadcasting or using any sort of commercial music on an AUDIO tape or in a video. Music in any production has to be logged with all details. PRODUCTION MUSIC provides a straightforward way to use a very large library of music from many different companies at reasonable cost and with copyright cleared with one licence.

The details in the table on the following page must be logged for any broadcast or commercial use of music in a media product. Copies of this form can then be distributed to the various copyright collection agencies.

MUTE   Means silent and refers to a recording where no SOUND has been recorded. Some shots are recorded as mute on purpose because the sound will be put on later, or perhaps for a technical reason. It should always be noted in the LOG if a SHOT is mute. *See Actuality, Recordist, Microphone.*

Production company Broadcaster
Production title Producer's name
CD no. CD title
CD label/record company
Track no. Track title
Artist
Composer Author/lyricist
Arranger Producer
Publisher
Duration used
Transmission time & channel
Digital/cable/satellite/terrestrial
Number of copies to be made
Countries for distribution

Sample blank music copyright form

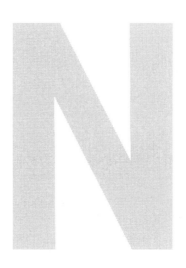

NAB National Association of Broadcasters. American organisation that agrees technical standards for the industry.

NAGRA Company name for a high-QUALITY, portable, AUDIO tape recorder, used to record SOUND on all types of media productions. Started by making industry-standard reel-to-reel tape recorders. Now makes, among a variety of audio recorders, a state-of-the-art 24-bit hard-disk recorder used on film and drama productions.

NAME SUPER Name superimposition. A standard TV method of naming the person appearing on the screen. The name is created by a CAPTION generator and SUPERIMPOSED over the person's image in the lower third of the screen. The style, FONT and size of the text is up to the individual programme. Some programmes put the name in a box or use colour backgrounds. *See Aston.*

NARRATION Words spoken by an out-of-vision (OOV) voice that explains or adds meaning to the pictures on the screen. Can be telling a story or reading COMMENTARY.

NEG Short for film negative. Films are SHOT on negative celluloid film. Images on the negative have to be converted to a positive PRINT in order to be viewed as originally shot. The print can then be projected in a cinema or converted to a video FORMAT via TELECINE. *See Neg Cutting.*

NEGATIVE Film negative. *See Neg.*

NEGATIVE CHECKS If a character in a drama is named by his or her full name, this has to be checked to see if there is anybody living with the same name who is well known or similar in characteristics such as age, height and colour. A fictional character has a negative check if no living person corresponds to the character's description and name.

NEG CUTTING NEGATIVE cutting. The film loaded into a film camera is negative film. The RUSHES or DAILIES are ungraded PRINTS of the negative. These ungraded prints are used to edit the film. When the film has gone through all the stages of EDITING and a FINE CUT has been agreed, the original negative is cut by specialist companies to match, frame by frame, the edited fine cut. This will then become the final neg cut version of the film and is ready to print for TRANSMISSION or showing in a cinema. *See Answer Print, Editing, Post-production.*

NEUTRAL DENSITY (ND) A type of camera FILTER that fits into the MATTEBOX, or filter holder, in front of the **LENS**, or is integrated into the design of a camcorder. This type of filter is used to cut down the brightness of the light, but not change the colour temperature. Handy for **EXTERIOR** shots in bright sunlight such as when shooting the traditional white buildings on a typical Greek island.

NEWS   The gathering of new facts and information about events in the world that impact on our lives and are of interest to us. News needs to be both relevant and of interest to a reader, viewer or listener. News in the media is highly selective and revolves around agreed news values. This is a way of sorting out which news to cover and which to reject. News is selected if it is important, dramatic, happens close to home, is new or unusual, is contentious or if it has immediate relevance, e.g. a natural disaster, such as an earthquake, would fulfil many of these criteria. News for broadcasting or publication in a newspaper is selected and organised in a newsroom by a news editor, with help from sub-editors and a team of journalists. For news to have greater impact in the media, a **REPORTER** will be sent to the scene of the event. A news reporter will attempt to establish what has happened, and when and where it happened. It may also be relevant to establish who was involved in the event, how it happened and why.

NEWS BULLETIN   TV, Radio. Current **NEWS** stories read by a **NEWSREADER**, with or without taped **INSERTS** or **LIVE** links, usually less than five minutes, after which it becomes a news programme or just 'the news'.

NEWSGROUP   Discussion group on the internet. People with shared interests can read and send comments for the whole group to see and respond to. Net users have the choice of a very wide variety of newsgroups on different subjects, where they can contribute their own ideas and views, and communicate with other users. Fans of Madonna, plane-spotters and skydiving enthusiasts all have their own newsgroups. Look for them via a **SEARCH ENGINE**. To send and receive messages, a 'reader' is required. The popular software for sending emails, Outlook Express, has a built-in newsgroup reader.

NEWSREADER   Person who reads the **NEWS** on TV or radio. On TV, has to be able to read **AUTOCUE**. Modern television channels employ journalists as newsreaders who can do **INTERVIEWS** and have input into the creation of the news. *See Eng, News Bulletin.*

NG   Shorthand often seen in a **PA's** log. Means the **SHOT** or **TAKE** is 'No Good' or not useable.

NICAM   Audio. Near instantaneous companded audio multiplex. Developed by BBC engineers and, in 1986, agreed by the government as the standard for UK stereo broadcasts. Subsequently recommended for terrestrial television broadcasts in Europe and adopted by home video recorder (**VHS**) manufacturers. Delivers high-quality **DIGITAL** sound to domestic TV sets. Nearly all terrestrial TV programmes are now recorded and transmitted in NICAM stereo.

NMK   New Media Knowledge www.nmk.co.uk Organisation that runs a programme of events, courses, seminars, research and publications for new media professionals. Works as a business and information resource for companies and individuals working in **INTERACTIVE**

digital media, e.g. courses on pitching for new media business, starting a new media business or successful freelancing.

NODDIES SHOTS of a PRESENTER, REPORTER or INTERVIEWER nodding as if listening intently to what the INTERVIEWEE is saying. Shot MUTE after the INTERVIEW has been carried out so that the EDITOR has something to CUT AWAY to when editing the interview.

NOISE Generally used to describe unwanted lines, dots or white streaks, or other visual disturbance, as seen on a TV MONITOR. Caused by electrical interference or possibly DROPOUT or some other problem on the VIDEOTAPE.

NON-LINEAR EDITING Computer video EDITING. All the material SHOT on video can be loaded onto a computer HARD DISK, via a DIGITAL link such as FIREWIRE or a USB port, and edited using suitable software such as ADOBE PREMIERE or AVID. The process is non-linear because picture and SOUND can be accessed separately, and each FRAME or SCENE can be viewed, moved or rearranged easily and quickly in any order. The sequence can be altered, copied or changed indefinitely, without losing the original RUSHES, and with no deterioration in technical QUALITY. Video effects, such as DISSOLVES and WIPES, can be added and any number of versions created. Depending on the power of the computer and the type of software, a 30-minute TV programme or 90-minute FEATURE film can be edited. The SOUNDTRACK can be mixed, TITLES and CREDIT sequences created, and the whole project RENDERED and copied to a video recorder. Most large projects will need extra work in POST-PRODUCTION before being ready for broadcasting, but smaller projects can be finalised in an Avid suite. *See Editing, Dub, Final Cut Pro, Digital.*

NTSC National Television Standards Committee (US). Adopted in 1953 as the standard television colour system for the US. Also in use in some countries in South America and Japan. *See PAL, SECAM.*

NUJ National Union of Journalists, Acorn House, 314 Gray's Inn Road, London WC1X 8DP www.gn.apc.org/media/ The largest union for journalists, RESEARCHERS and EDITORS working on NEWS and current affairs radio and TV programmes and newspapers.

OB Outside Broadcast. The televising of an event that is outside the **STUDIO**, using a **MULTI-CAMERA** set-up. Each of several cameras sends pictures (and **SOUND**) to a **SCANNER** vehicle on site. The OB **DIRECTOR**, working from a small TV **GALLERY** set up in the scanner, selects the pictures, working as the **VISION MIXER**, for **LIVE** transmission or recording. An OB unit has its own power source and is able to relay broadcast-**QUALITY** pictures back to base for live transmission for an event like horse-racing. Radio also uses outside broadcast units to relay sound back to base from a live event.

OBJECTIVITY The aim of objectivity in **NEWS** reporting is to remain neutral and give fair coverage to all sides of an argument, without favouring any particular party. Public service broadcasters, such as the BBC, and some commercial broadcasters, strive to maintain objectivity in all programmes, but particularly in news and current affairs. News-gathering agencies such as Reuters and ITN, have gained international credibility for factual integrity and the objectivity of their reports. The BBC World Service is recognised throughout the world for its objectivity and impartiality on world affairs.

OBSCENITY Taste and what causes offence to the public changes with time. Very bad language, explicit depiction of sexual intercourse or other controversial activities, broadcast on radio or television, may upset listeners or viewers. They may complain to the broadcaster or to a broadcasting watchdog, such as the **BROADCASTING STANDARDS** council. It is an offence under the Obscene Publications Act to broadcast anything that would 'tend to deprave and corrupt', but this is notoriously difficult to define. All broadcasters have agreed standards of what can and cannot be seen on TV, particularly before the **WATERSHED**. *See Taste and Decency.*

OFFICIAL SECRETS ACT Section two of this act was passed in 1989 and can cause concern to journalists. It concerns crime, defence, security and intelligence, special investigation and the interception of letters and communications, as well as communications between government and international agencies. Journalists must be careful that what they publish or broadcast in these areas does not contravene the Act. *See D-Notice.*

OFFLINE EDIT A low-cost form of video **EDITING** that uses copies of the original pictures to make a **ROUGH CUT** or early non-broadcastable version of a programme. **NON-LINEAR** computer editing can also be offline with the same result. The rough cut can be shown to a client or **EDITOR** and, after adjustments to the programme, an **EDL** is created. This is a computer disk with the data of all the edit decisions made in the offline. This can be taken to an **ONLINE EDIT**, where the high-quality original pictures can be conformed, using data from the EDL to create a broadcast-quality final version.

OFF MIC Occurs when a speaker or actor's voice, or other **SOUND** source, is outside the sensitive pick-up area of a **MICROPHONE** usually because the mic is not close enough to the sound source. The voice sounds thin and far away, or can hardly be heard at all, and is said to be off mic.

OFF THE RECORD Useful information offered to journalists and **RESEARCHERS** by government officials, company employees and members of other organisations that is definitely not for broadcast, but may help as background to a **NEWS** story. *See **On the Record**.*

OMNIDIRECTIONAL MIC **MICROPHONE** that can pick up **SOUND** from all directions in a circle of 360 degrees around the sensitive area of the mic. *See **Cardioid**.*

ON AIR A lit-up 'On Air' sign on a door indicates that the **STUDIO** or work area behind the door is broadcasting or recording **LIVE**. It is a warning that you should not make a noise and must definitely not barge into the studio. To get an **ITEM** on air means to get it broadcast.

ONLINE Internet. When hooked up to the internet via a phone line and through an ISP, you are online. With a **BROADBAND** connection you could be permanently online and have a fast connection.

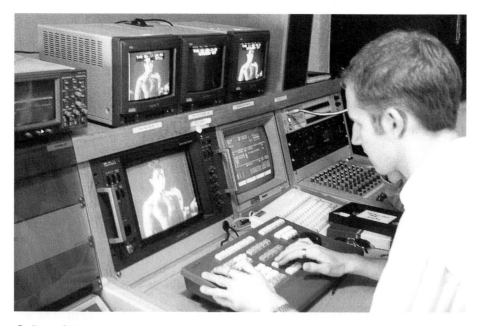

Online editing

ONLINE EDIT   Highest-quality EDITING of VIDEOTAPES in a dedicated editing suite, often in a FACILITY HOUSE where video effects, CAPTIONS, CREDITS and other visuals are added. A PRODUCER of a TV commercial may take the programme tapes straight into an online edit suite to create the final edit MASTER. For a longer programme, an OFFLINE EDIT will have produced an EDL that can then be conformed in an online edit.

ON LOCATION   Refers to the fact that the production of a media product is taking place at a site that is not a STUDIO or the production office. *See Location*.

ON SCREEN   If something in a moving-image production is on screen, then the AUDIENCE can see it. It has definitely been recorded as part of the finished product. In print, refers to page layout that is created on a computer.

ON THE RECORD   Information provided by the government or an organisation, often at a press conference or during an INTERVIEW, that may be broadcast or printed. *See Embargo, Off the Record*.

OOV   Out Of Vision. Anyone that cannot be seen by the camera is OOV, although the MICROPHONE could still be open, so be careful what you say about the DIRECTOR! OOV in a SCRIPT indicates that the following words will not be spoken on camera.

OPERATOR   Person who operates television or film equipment, e.g. a video recorder or TELECINE, as opposed to a technician, who maintains or repairs equipment. An engineer designs and constructs equipment. Broadcasting companies may employ engineers to repair and maintain equipment. *See Camera Operator*.

OPTICAL   Film. A visual effect created after the film has been processed. This can be something quite straightforward, such as a DISSOLVE, or a complex multi-screen effect. The effect is created by an optical printer.

OSCILLOSCOPE   Test equipment that displays information on a screen. Used, typically, to show how a television picture looks electronically.

OUT CUE   The last few words of a taped TV or radio story or a LIVE contribution, which are written on the CUE SHEET or have been previously agreed. This is so the PRESENTER knows when the tape has ended and can move on to the next item, and the studio technicians know when to FADE OUT that particular SOUND source. TV reports also have a visual out cue written on the cue sheet describing the last pictures on the tape.

OUT OF FOCUS   Picture that is not sharp and crystal clear. Seen through the VIEWFINDER of a video, film or still camera, the subject appears fuzzy or 'soft', and not sharp and clear. It is not in focus. Refocus manually or by using AUTO-FOCUS. Sometimes a DIRECTOR will shoot a SCENE and make the subject(s) slightly soft, usually for a romantic effect.

OUT OF SYNC   When the picture and the SOUNDTRACK do not run in unison and people appear to move their lips before or after the words are heard. The SOUND is not IN SYNC with the pictures.

OUTPUT   All the programmes, commercials, TRAILS, LINKS, in fact, everything transmitted by a particular radio or TV station, are known collectively as the output.

OUTSIDE BROADCAST   *See OB.*

OUT-TAKES   Unusable filmed material. Occasionally, can be one of those excruciating moments from films or TV programmes when well-known actors forget their lines or PRESENTERS fall over the set. The basis for a raft of broadcast programmes linked by some very unfunny scripts.

OVERHEADS   General term, meaning the cost of items that do not appear directly in the BUDGET of a programme or film. These might include the total cost of running a production office, including phone rental, heating, electricity, fax paper and computer maintenance.

OVERHEAD SHOT   SHOT taken by a camera that is located above the ACTION and looks down on the action as if from a rooftop. The camera may be on a CRANE or CHERRY PICKER or in a HELICOPTER.

OVERLAY   In television, the combining of two picture sources to make one composite picture. This is done on a video-mixing console, using a switching signal from one of the sources. There are many uses for an overlay, including adding GRAPHICS such as a NAME SUPER onto a moving picture. *See Chromakey, Gallery, Wipe.*

PA Production Assistant. Works closely with the PRODUCER and the DIRECTOR in the preparation of SCRIPTS, with research and all the other paperwork. ON LOCATION, does the SHOT LIST and can look after CONTINUITY, as well as keeping the BUDGET. In a TV STUDIO, works closely with the studio director on creating the script, and keeps a running commentary on the SHOT number and what camera is on what shot at any time during REHEARSAL and recording. Also counts down into and out of tape INSERTS, counts out of INTERVIEWS and keeps total running time of the PROGRAMME – a very busy but rewarding job.

PACT Producers Alliance for Cinema and Television, 45 Mortimer Street, London W1N 7TD www.pact.co.uk Association for independent TV and film PRODUCERS and independent PRODUCTION companies in the UK. Provides information and a consultancy service, and organises training for members. Provides advice on negotiating deals and CONTRACTS. Monthly magazine, *PACT,* essential reading for the independent broadcast and film sector.

PAL Phase Alternate Line. The British colour television standard system with 625 lines. Also the standard in much of Europe (except France), and Australia and New Zealand, but not in the US or Japan. *See NTSC, Secam.*

PAN Smooth camera movement in a horizontal arc from left to right or right to left. Needs to be done on a TRIPOD or DOLLY. Often used to follow a moving object or person. Difficult to shoot in one liquid movement. Overused by tourists with camcorders at famous sites leading to boring holiday videos that are difficult to edit. *See Crab, Shot Size, Tilt Up/Down.*

PAN & TILT HEAD Special camera mounting on the top of a TRIPOD, PEDESTAL or CRANE that allows the camera to move smoothly up and down in a vertical plane (TILT) and sideways in a horizontal plane (PAN) in either direction. *See Crab, Shot Size.*

PANTOGRAPH In a TV STUDIO, a device with crossed metal arms, from which to hang a LUMINAIRE, so that it can be moved up and down. Normally has an electric motor that allows remote operation but in smaller studios it can be moved by hand.

PARABOLIC MIC MICROPHONE mounting that looks like a small shiny bowl with a mic in the middle. Used to pick up a specific distant SOUND source at a sports OB or similar. *See Microphones.*

PARALLEL PORT Computer. A 25-pin socket that connects PERIPHERALS to a computer – most commonly a PRINTER. *See USB, Firewire.*

Motorised pantograph

PASTE-UP Print. The way a page will look before it goes to the printers. A DUMMY draft of the page with all the COPY, photographs and artwork pasted onto a sheet of card to look like the final product. *See Layout.*

PAY-OFF The final SCENES in a film that finish the story and tie up all the loose ends. It can surprise the AUDIENCE, possibly by a twist in the plot. Also colloquial for final goodbyes from a TV presenter at the end of a programme.

Print. The final paragraphs of an ARTICLE that can wrap up all the loose ends or just make a satisfying conclusion.

PAY PER VIEW   Multimedia. System based on digital TRANSMISSION that offers consumers the opportunity to select and view a film at any time of the day or night. Service offered by DIGITAL cable and satellite channels. Cost is similar to renting a VHS or DVD from a high-street video rental shop. Also available with suitable software on the internet.

PBU   Photo Blow-Up. Name for a very big enlargement of a photograph used as part of the set in a TV STUDIO. Typically, PBUs of famous politicians are used to form the set in a current affairs programme.

PDA   Personal Digital Assistant. Refers to those small electronic portable personal organisers made by companies such as Psion and Palm. These are small portable computers that can do almost as much as a desktop computer, and they are becoming more sophisticated all the time. Typically, a PDA will have an electronic diary, calendar, address book, mobile phone access, word processing, internet access, EMAIL and other software, as well as a variety of games. Some utilise BLUETOOTH technology, which can set up a wireless link to a computer or phone.

PEDESTAL (PED)   A wheeled mount for a STUDIO camera, operated by a CAMERAMAN, that can raise the camera (ELEVATE) or lower it (DEPRESS), and can move from side to side (CRAB) or go forwards (TRACK in) or backwards (track out). Standard mounting for a TV studio camera as it is so flexible and can do smooth tracking shots on a properly laid studio floor. *See Crane, Dolly, Tripod.*

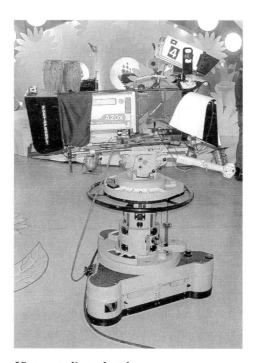

Vinten studio pedestal

PER DIEM   Small amount of money paid each day ('diem' is Latin for day) to cast and CREW on a film production while on LOCATION. The money is to cover costs of drinks, meals and everyday sundries that are not covered by the CONTRACT. *See Budget, Contributor's Agreement.*

PERIPHERAL   Computer. Peripherals are additional equipment or accessories that can be connected to the computer, either through a PARALLEL PORT or USB. A peripheral can be a keyboard, PRINTER, SCANNER or a removable storage device such as a ZIP drive.

PERMITS   Permission forms. Any special form that has to be filled in to allow filming to happen. A production company needs permission to use virtually any LOCATION or to film in a public place. *See Contributor's Agreement, Release Form.*

PHANTOM POWER   The DC power supply to certain types of MICROPHONE, which appears to come from nowhere (phantom), as it uses the mic cable. Some mics need a separate power line.

PHONE-IN   Name for a TV or radio programme or part of a programme that has broadcast input from members of the public via telephone.

PhotoShop   Adobe PhotoShop is a very popular industry-standard graphics-editing software package. Combines drawing tools with layer design features that offer a wide range of creative options. Has razor-sharp text and shapes and a useful web tool kit. Version 6.0 includes the new ImageReady 3.0 software for advanced web processing. Has text-warping and image-distortion tools to manipulate any text or picture though a large range of creative options.

PICTURE EDITOR   Another name for a video EDITOR. In TV NEWS, a picture editor works to a journalist or news editor and so has less editorial control over the pictures he or she is editing than a traditional film or video editor.

PILOT (PROGRAMME)   One-off programme made by a TV or radio production company. The point of making a pilot is usually to sell to a broadcaster a series based on this one-off programme. Broadcasters can and do commission and pay for a wide variety of pilot programmes, including children's programmes, comedy, entertainment and dramas. They are always looking for a show that will attract high ratings, but sometimes, if you have a stunning idea, you have to make your own pilot with your own cash.

PITCHING   Refers to the way a production company or an individual tries to sell an idea to a broadcaster, advertising company, film company or movie STUDIO. The aim is to make the organisation see that your film idea or programme concept is truly wonderful and worth spending vast amounts on financing or at least putting up the cash for DEVELOPMENT or even a PILOT.

PIXEL   Photography, video. The tiny dots on the TV screen that deliver the picture are, in fact, a grid of coloured electronic squares called pixels. Also, part of the technology that makes up a DIGITAL CAMERA or video camera where there may be over a million pixels to create an image. The more pixels, the better the picture RESOLUTION. The number of pixels on a television screen is related to how many vertical and horizontal lines the signal has. The UK, Australian and European transmission system, PAL, has 625 lines with 403,200 pixels. The US NTSC system has 307,200 pixels. *See CCD, Frame Rate, Secam, Format.*

PLAGIARISM   Literary theft. The stealing of someone else's written words and ideas and making them seem your own. The lifting of chunks of text from someone else's published or COPYRIGHTED work and putting them in a SCRIPT or literary work that has your name as the author. This is illegal and protected by law. *See Copyright.*

PLASMA DISPLAY MONITOR   A plasma display monitor, or panel, is an ultra-thin, perfectly flat WIDESCREEN television set. It has a clear, very high-RESOLUTION picture, removing most of the reflections and distortions found in a conventional television and giving a wider viewing angle. It can be hung on a wall or from a ceiling, offering big-screen home cinema without the need for a bulky projector. It works on a different principle to a conventional TV set and does not contain a CATHODE RAY TUBE. The PIXELS are activated differently. Each pixel is made up of tiny phosphor-coated, low-pressure glass cavities, which contain a gas or plasma that is a mixture of neon and xenon. Behind these cavities are coloured phosphors, one red, one blue and one green for each cavity. An electrical signal heats the gas, and ultraviolet rays are emitted. These ultraviolet rays strike the red, green and blue phosphors on the back glass of the display, causing them to produce visible light and create an image on the screen. *See HDTV.*

PLAYBACK   The reproduction of recorded vision and SOUND, or sound only, from electronic recording equipment such as a camera, video recorder or CD player. Modern DIGITAL sound, which is stored on a CD or received via digital TRANSMISSION, is converted to ANALOGUE so that it can be heard through a television set, headphones or a loudspeaker.

PLAY LIST   List of commercial music discs selected to be played on a particular radio station. Can change weekly or daily.

PLUGGER   Person who has the job of promoting new commercial music recordings (particularly CD singles) to broadcasters, PRESENTERS and club DJs, in order to get maximum exposure of these new recordings on the radio and in the clubs.

PLUG-IN   Multimedia. Software that increases the effectiveness of a web browser. Plug-in software enables the browser to show ANIMATIONS, view video CLIPS and play back SOUND, e.g. RealPlayer.

POP 3   Multimedia. Post Office Protocol 3. The main protocol used by an ISP to send and receive EMAIL.

POPS   Refers to MICROPHONE pops. DISTORTION of the sound from a microphone caused by a PRESENTER speaking too close to the mic, making a pop-like sound. Can be largely avoided by putting a plastic foam windshield over the mic, sometimes called a pop sock.

PORTAL   Multimedia. Refers to a website that acts as a door or gateway leading to a whole range of services and content offered by the portal provider on the internet.

PORTRAIT   Print. Refers to the way a page, graphic or picture is aligned. Describes a page set-up that is rectangular, but longer vertically than horizontally. It is higher (longer vertically) than it is wide. The other way to refer to how a page is aligned is **LANDSCAPE**. This is wider (longer horizontally) than it is high, typically in the ratio of 4:3.

Portrait page layout

POST-MODERN FRAMING   Way of using the camera to frame a SHOT to create visual excitement or humour, often by using extreme CLOSE-UPS of a person's face in an INTERVIEW or with unusual camera ANGLES and video effects. The flexibility of a high-QUALITY, lightweight, DIGITAL CAMERA allows the operator to be very imaginative in framing shots or putting the camera in unusual positions. The pictures can then be manipulated in POST-PRODUCTION to create a variety of effects that allegedly keep the viewer watching. The essence of post-modernism in filming is to borrow ideas from a number of earlier sources and amalgamate them, referencing previous televisual ideas, artistic movements and movies. This is sometimes exemplified visually by references to an aspect of Picasso's portrait painting that concentrates on emphasising an ear or an eye. This type of extreme close-up is then used in an interview. Other references come from areas of surrealism.

POST-PRODUCTION The process that takes place after all the relevant material for a radio or TV programme or film has been shot, leading finally to completion of the project. For a moving-image product, this is mainly the editing of the pictures and SOUND. Also includes the sound DUB, creating TITLES and CREDITS, and adding any video effects or CGI sequences. In film, the process includes NEG CUTTING, OPTICAL effects that are made in the LABS, and making a SHOW PRINT of the film that is ready for broadcasting or distribution.

POST-SYNCHING The adding or replacing of matching SOUND to the sound that has already been recorded on LOCATION. This is usually DIALOGUE that is re-recorded by the same actors in a DUBBING THEATRE to be in LIP SYNC with the pictures. Much of the dialogue in a movie is recreated this way for better performances and better technical QUALITY for the SOUNDTRACK.

POV Point Of View. The SHOT that shows what a character in a film is actually seeing from where he or she is standing. Often used in a horror film to suggest what a monster is able to see through its slit eyes, or the view the hero actually sees, hanging from the edge of a skyscraper when he looks down. A POV shot in a DOCUMENTARY might be HAND-HELD to suggest what a CONTRIBUTOR is seeing as he or she climbs a mountain or rescues someone at sea.

PPL Phonographic Performance Ltd, 1 Upper James Street, London W1R 1LB www.ppluk.com PPL licenses the public performance and broadcasting of SOUND recordings. It represents over 2400 record companies and performers, and issues licences for the public performance of commercial records. The licence fees, after deduction of running costs, are distributed to the record company members and performers.

PPM Peak Programme Meter. A meter on a SOUND MIXING DESK, typically in a radio STUDIO, designed to show the volume of sound output from a FADER. The meter shows the peak value of a signal level. Shows the peaks of electrical activity, indicating peaks and levels of sound, allowing the operator to adjust and balance sound levels in a programme. The numbers on a PPM run from one to seven. The interval between each number is four decibels (dB). The number six corresponds to 100 per cent MODULATION of a transmitter. Any level over that is likely to DISTORT the sound. When balancing a speech and music programme it is generally considered that speech should peak at 5½ and music at 4–4½ on the PPM.

PRE-FADE Audio. A way of listening to the OUTPUT of a channel on a SOUND MIXING DESK before opening the FADER itself. This is a way of setting the level of the output of the channel and listening to the content without opening the fader and mixing its output into the programme. Useful for setting up a disc on a LIVE radio show. In radio, also means starting the closing music or SIG TUNE at an agreed time in the programme, but not fading it up. When the speech stops, the music is faded up and comes to an end at exactly the right time for the end of the programme, e.g. if the closing music is 30 seconds in DURATION and a live programme ends at 11a.m., the music will be pre-faded at 10.59:30 to end exactly at 11.00:00.

PRE-PRODUCTION The process and period of time during which all aspects of the planning and preparation of a TV programme or film take place. From initial idea through the SCRIPT-writing process, to getting a production team together and the very important issue of raising the finance, all come under pre-production. Basically, it is getting everything ready to start **PRODUCTION**, which means shooting. In movie production, there is an even earlier process, revolving around developing a final version of the script and finding the finance to make the movie, called in-development. *See Development.*

PRESENTER Person who introduces a radio or TV programme. May or may not be well known or an expert in a subject. Appears in vision to introduce a TV programme. Links ITEMS on radio. Needs to be able to talk to camera and read **AUTOCUE** and/or memorise lines of SCRIPT, as well as conduct INTERVIEWS. *See Anchor, Reporter.*

PRESS RELEASE Printed information provided by an individual or company and issued to the press to try to generate press interest in the products or activities promoted in the release.

PREVIEW

a) The showing to a selected AUDIENCE of a programme or film before TRANSMISSION or theatrical release to a general audience.

b) In a TV STUDIO, it means to view a picture or tape INSERT before it is transmitted or recorded. A colour MONITOR in the GALLERY is set up as a preview monitor. This allows the DIRECTOR to view what is about to be recorded or go out LIVE, particularly a composite SHOT that has been created through the VISION MIXING DESK.

PRIME TIME TV. Refers to the time of day that attracts the largest viewing AUDIENCES on a TV channel or largest listening audience on a radio station. For a terrestrial TV channel, such as BBC1, this is mid-evening, from about 1930hrs to 2200hrs. *See BARB, RAJAR.*

PRINT Film. The positive version of a film taken from the NEGATIVE. This is the version that is projected in a cinema.

Photography. A picture that has been taken from a negative and printed onto photographic paper, and may be reproduced in a printed publication.

Multimedia. Means to download text or pictures from a computer file onto a HARD COPY format such as paper.

PRINTER Computer. Device that prints DIGITAL data, such as files, artwork and pictures, from a computer. The two main technologies are INKJET and laser. Both can print in colour and black and white. Printer QUALITY is expressed in RESOLUTION, measured in DOTS PER INCH (dpi).

PRINT IT! DIRECTOR's or PRODUCER's comment during or at the end of editing, indicating an item or whole programme, or a publication, is now just right and needs nothing more doing to it, and can be 'printed'.

PRIVACY An individual has the right, under the European Human Rights Act, to respect for his or her private and family life, home and correspondence. People working in print, television and radio need to respect an individual's right to privacy, however famous he or she might be, and make sure they do not fall foul of the law. It is important to obtain an individual's permission before recording pictures or an INTERVIEW. *See Copyright, Libel, Release Form.*

PROCESSOR   Computer. The electronic chip that is the driving force of a computer, the best-known brand name being Intel.

PRODUCER   The organisational and administrative head of a production team, who has the ultimate responsibility to get the film, TV or radio programme completed and ON AIR.

In film, the producer also sets up the financing of a film and may then leave everything to the DIRECTOR, or take a more hands-on approach to the day-to-day running of the film's production. In TV, the producer initiates the idea for a programme and then follows it through from PRE-PRODUCTION to PREVIEWS and TRANSMISSION. In FACTUAL PROGRAMMING, he or she may also direct some of the material and will be involved in the EDITING. Also responsible for keeping the programme under BUDGET, hiring and firing personnel and making sure things happen when they are supposed to, as well as coping with the many things that get in the way of a smooth production. *See Film Producer, TV Producer.*

PRODUCTION

a) The process and the period of time in making a film, TV or radio programme, when nearly everything has been set up, filming is taking place and material is being recorded. This is the period for a moving-image product after PRE-PRODUCTION, where SOUND and visual material are acquired so that the POST-PRODUCTION process can take place.

b) Name for a media product such as a TV or radio programme or a theatre show.

c) Generic name for the non-technical personnel working on a media project who get the show together, includes the PRODUCER and the DIRECTOR, e.g. 'production will be down later with the final SCRIPT'.

PRODUCTION ASSISTANT   *See PA.*

PRODUCTION MUSIC   Music that has been commissioned, composed, performed and recorded especially for television and AUDIO productions, such as advertisements, broadcast programmes, film and video productions. It is available from companies such as Chappell or Bruton, who offer libraries of CDs, catalogued under helpful titles such as gothic horror, rap, classical themes or mean streets. The value of production music is that there are no copyright difficulties. The MCPS issues a licence that covers all the rights required to include that work in your production, whether it is for broadcasting or a corporate video. All the rights belonging to each recording have been 'bought out' by the company. This music can be cleared for world TRANSMISSION and paid for at a reasonable set rate by obtaining a licence from the MCPS. *See Copyright, Music Copyright, PRS, PPL.*

PRODUCTION VALUES   Refers to the overall perceived QUALITY of a media product. A quality product is deemed to have high production values, whereas a less professional product is likely to have low production values. For a moving-image production, this includes everything from star actors in the cast to the FORMAT in which it is produced – high-definition video or DIGITAL BETACAM offer very high quality. A Hollywood feature film generally has high production values. It is shot on 35mm film, has at least one A-list actor and millions of dollars invested in it. The high production values should be obvious to the viewer in terms of glossy LOCATIONS, daredevil stunts and impressive SPECIAL EFFECTS. A lower-BUDGET film, with good actors, an experienced DIRECTOR and a terrific SCRIPT can still have high production values. These will be evident in the quality of the storytelling, the overall standard of the acting, the imaginative use of the camera, and other subtler reasons, rather than the number of special effects.

PROOF(S)   Print. A trial copy of a photograph, graphic or printed text that is sent to the PRODUCTION team. All aspects of the product can then be checked for STYLE, spelling mistakes and any other errors, and to make sure that it has been created in accordance with the original brief. First proofs are typeset copies of the text before corrections and alterations. Final proofs are typeset copies of the corrected text with illustrations and pictures, which go back to the production team for a final check.

PROOFREADING   Refers to printed texts. The checking of text PROOFS for content, grammar, spelling mistakes and any other errors or omissions.

PROPS   Short for properties. Theatrical term, taken up by TV and film, for any portable item that is seen in SHOT or is handled by an actor or PRESENTER on a TV or film set. Can be something small, such as a handbag, an umbrella, or a gun, or a larger item, such as a coffin or a dustbin to hide in. Some props, such as a telephone, may actually work and are FULLY PRAC. Others are just set-dressing and are non-practical.

PRS   Performing Rights Society, 29–33 Berners Street, London W1P 4AA www.prs.co.uk Non-profit-making membership organisation for writers and publishers of COPYRIGHTED music. Collects licence fees from music users and places where LIVE and recorded music is heard, and distributes the fees as ROYALTIES to its members. The PRS collects fees from clubs, pubs, shops and concert venues, as well as broadcasting companies with whom it usually has blanket agreements.

PSC   Portable Single Camera. Somewhat dated term used to describe the use of a video camcorder with a CAMERAMAN working in the field, particularly for acquiring NEWS footage. *See ENG.*

PTC   Piece To Camera. A TV PRESENTER speaking and looking straight into the camera LENS and directly addressing the viewer is doing a piece to camera. Typically viewed on NEWS, entertainment, and current affairs and factual programmes. *See Autocue, Newsreader.*

PUBLIC SERVICE BROADCASTING   Radio and TV programmes provided by a public service broadcaster for the benefit of the public, and not run commercially to make a profit. In the UK, the BBC runs all its services for television and radio as a public service broadcaster. It is entirely independent of the government and operates outside its control. It is financed by a licence fee that all households with a TV receiver are required to pay each year. In the US, public service broadcasting is provided by organisations that are funded by state grants and subscriptions from listeners and viewers. Many countries in Europe and throughout the world have public service networks that are jointly funded by a licence fee and advertising.

PULL FOCUS   Refers to the way a film or video camera can be used to change the FOCUS within one SHOT. Typically, a pull focus set-up involves a TWO-SHOT, where there is DIALOGUE between two characters. One character is in FOCUS in the FOREGROUND and the other character is OUT OF FOCUS in the background. As the foreground character stops speaking, the CAMERA assistant turns the focus ring on the camera to a previously marked limit, to throw the foreground character out of focus and the background character into focus. This can emphasise psychological distance between the characters or be used for visual effect.

PUNDIT   Colloquial for a programme CONTRIBUTOR who can talk fluently and with knowledge and understanding on a particular subject. *See Contributor.*

PUP   A small spotlight used on a film or TV set, usually 750 watts.

PYROTECHNICS   Explosions or use of explosive materials. Any use of explosive materials, including fireworks, on a set must be set up and operated by trained pyrotechnics personnel.

QUALITY   Refers to extremely high standards in all areas, in reference to all the elements in a media product, whether it is print, radio or moving image. Quality does not just refer to very high technical standards, although these are most important. High technical quality is always required by broadcasting organisations. It also refers to everything else, from the STYLE and structure of the SCREENPLAY to the final edit. Film companies strive for exceptionally high standards of technical sophistication in terms of the clarity, colour and RESOLUTION of the picture, and FREQUENCY, range and richness of the acoustic experience (*see Dolby*). Quality also refers to PRODUCTION VALUES, where the very best work is sought in all areas, from direction to POST-PRODUCTION. A quality product means the very highest standards, from script to screen or from pen to product.

QuarkXpress   Multimedia. Trade name for print industry-standard software for creating magazine-style pages on a computer, including catalogues, newsletters and newspapers. Can manipulate text, pictures and GRAPHICS on the screen to a house design or to conform to the LAYOUT of the magazine. Text can be directly input to a page and pictures enlarged or wrapped around text. A flexible system that allows considerable creativity for EDITORS, SUB-EDITORS and journalists, from original idea to final output.

QUESTIONS   *See Interview Questions.*

QUIZ QUESTIONS   Written by specialist freelance question setters. Each quiz show creates its own style and FORMAT of questions that has to be strictly adhered to. For the top-money quiz shows, each question and its answer has to be checked against at least three different published sources.

R

RACKS   TV. Personnel working in racks MONITOR and regulate the vision signals between cameras and the studio GALLERY. They make sure that all cameras in a MULTI-CAMERA set-up are sending pictures that are technically matching in terms of colour balance and resolution. A TV STUDIO complex will have a CONTROL ROOM with racks operators who can separately monitor picture QUALITY.

RADIO ACADEMY   5 Market Place, London W1N 7AH www.radacad.demon.co.uk Organisation for professionals working in the radio industry. Seeks to promote excellence throughout the industry. Hosts annual radio conference. Regional centres run meetings and workshops.

RADIO MIC   A wireless MICROPHONE. A hand-held radio mic has a built-in radio transmitter. A small lapel mic has no cable, but is attached to a small radio transmitter, often hooked to the belt of the actor. In a TV STUDIO, the mic sends SOUND to a receiver from where it goes by cable to the SOUND MIXING DESK. In the field, the receiver is attached to the camera, or is part of the sound recordist's kit. Several mics can be used on different radio FREQUENCIES, and their output mixed on a portable SOUND MIXER. Used extensively in drama PRODUCTION or by a PRESENTER. *See Audio.*

RAIN LOOP   A loop of video or film showing rain falling that can be continuously SUPERIMPOSED on a SCENE to give the effect of rain. Remember, the characters in the scene need to look wet as well!

RAJAR   Radio Joint Audience Research www.rajar.co.uk. Publishes quarterly listening figures for all radio stations in the UK. Established in 1992 to operate a single AUDIENCE measurement system for the radio industry. Measures audiences for BBC radio stations, UK licensed and other commercial stations. The company is wholly owned by the Commercial Radio Companies Association and by the BBC. Data is collected using a seven-day listening diary, filled in by approximately 130,000 respondents each year. They are asked to fill in all details of their radio listening for every quarter-hour between 6a.m. and midnight, and every half-hour between midnight and 6a.m. Every three months, RAJAR publishes an overview of the results, such as the average hours of listening and each radio station's share of all the broadcast hours in its area. It does not publish radio listening by programme for the stations. The fully itemised details are only available on subscription. *See BARB.*

RAM   Random Access Memory. The temporary memory section of a computer that saves data only while the computer is switched on. The computer puts current data in the RAM section so that it can be accessed quickly and randomly during use.

RATE CARD A list of prices produced by a commercial company offering media PRODUCTION services and equipment for hire. Services and kit for film and TV are costed by the hour, by the day or longer. A FACILITY HOUSE will offer EDITING and other POST-PRODUCTION services for DRY HIRE or with an operator. Many companies hire out equipment to TV programme-makers and filmmakers, as so much of it is very expensive to purchase outright.

RATINGS The measurement of the AUDIENCE for a mass media product. In the case of television, a rating for each TV channel is arrived at by a formula based on a sample of the audience – about 10,000 homes in the UK – compiled from electronic devices in the home that MONITOR viewing habits. Time-shift viewing, using a VCR, is also monitored. As more DIGITAL channels become available and viewing becomes fragmented, a larger sample or a more sophisticated system will be needed to obtain accurate results. For radio, the sample is made up of selected members of the audience who fill in a listening diary, giving details of what station they listen to at 15-minute intervals throughout the day. The rating for a particular programme is important for advertisers, who wish to know if their commercials are reaching a decent-sized audience. If not, they can argue for reduced rates from the TV channel. New and improved methods of measuring ratings for both radio and TV are being considered. So far, no method is absolutely accurate. Websites also have ratings based on the number of HITS. *See BARB, RAJAR.*

RDS Radio Data System. An inaudible data signal added to most FM radio TRANSMISSIONS throughout Europe. It allows radio stations to send additional information, such as the name of the station, reliable time data and news, with the standard radio programme signal. Motorists with a suitable RDS radio enjoy better reception and access to travel information. The system automatically finds the best transmitter and FREQUENCY for the selected station, eliminating the need to retune when passing from one transmitter to the next. *See DAB.*

REAL TIME The actual DURATION of an event or activity. Most programmes are edited and therefore compress real time. Events that happen in real time are of the same duration and run at the same speed as they would in real life. Also, refers to how long a piece of equipment will take to achieve some electronic activity, such as copying pictures and SOUND from VIDEOTAPE to videotape. To take real time means that it will take the actual duration of the ITEM and cannot be copied at a higher speed. *See Time Code.*

RECCE Derived from the French word reconnaissance, meaning a survey or discovery. For filmmakers, the recce is an essential part of PRE-PRODUCTION. It means a visit to a LOCATION, with the aim of finding out if it is suitable for filming for a particular programme. The DIRECTOR and the RESEARCHER normally carry out the recce. For drama, the LOCATION MANAGER and/or the PRODUCTION MANAGER accompany the director. Things to check for when on a recce range from the availability of electrical power, availability of parking and access by vehicles, to the direction of the sun and the lack of loud noise such as aircraft taking off. It is important to establish whether or not it is possible to get permission to film on the scheduled days. Every location, however small a part it may play in the script, should have a recce. It will be to the benefit of the film and could save an awful lot of trouble later. *See Contracts.*

RECORDING FORMATS   Electronic devices use a variety of different systems to achieve similar results. Broadly speaking, these are known as formats. In TV and radio, refers to the way pictures and **SOUND** are stored or recorded. Can be **ANALOGUE** tape, such as **BETACAM SP**, or ¼-inch tape for radio. The main **DIGITAL** formats include the **DV** family and **DIGITAL BETACAM**. There are over 20 different **VIDEOTAPE** recording formats available. Sound-only recording formats include the non-**COMPRESSED**, high-**QUALITY** digital tape format, **DAT**. **AUDIO** disc formats include MINIDISC, CD or HARD DISK.

RECORDING OFF AIR   Making a recording of a radio or TV programme directly from the **TRANSMISSION** of the programme rather than from a **MASTER** tape. Also known as **ROT** (Recording Off Transmission).

RECORDIST   Name for the sound recordist on a film or TV production.

RED-EYE REDUCTION   Photography. **DIGITAL** and film cameras with a built-in flash have this feature. When using a flash, the pupils in the subject's eyes tend to be coloured red on the film **PRINTS**. The flash bounces back off the red blood vessels in the retina of the eyes and causes this red-eye effect. To minimise this, the red-eye reduction fires off a short pre-flash that makes the subject's pupils reduce in size for a moment. When the larger flash fires almost immediately afterwards to take the picture, there is less area of the retina to bounce off.

REDHEAD   A lightweight, variable-beam 800-watt floodlight with an ability to **FOCUS** the light and vary it from **SPOT** to **FLOOD**, varying the beam from about 42 degrees to nearly 90

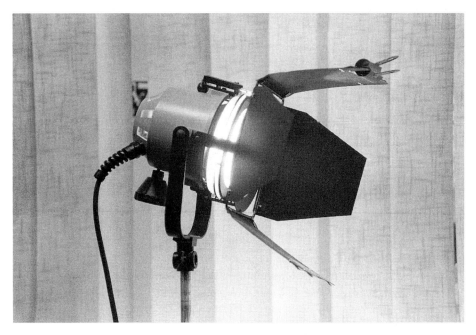

Redhead with barn doors

degrees. Very popular with **LOCATION** film **CREWS** working on **FACTUAL PROGRAMMES.** TV crews like to carry a redhead kit in a transportable case, with three or four lamps and their stands. This makes it possible to set up a **THREE-POINT LIGHTING** plan for filming on location. Other suitable location lights include a **BLONDE** and a **REFLECTOR.**

REFLECTOR

a) Flat device, with a very reflective surface, in silver, gold or white, which recycles light from a light source such as the sun or a film light. Delivers a relatively **SOFT LIGHT.** Can be made of strong, fold-up material and hand-held, or be larger and more rigid, with its own stand. A serviceable reflector can be a made out of a rigid sheet of white polystyrene, held up by clipping it onto a lighting stand. A reflector is a versatile way of lighting a subject when filming in sunny **LOCATIONS.**

b) As part of the mechanism of a film light, the reflector is the curved, shiny surface that concentrates the light's beam.

Reflector on a television drama location

REHEARSE/RECORD   A common method of video and **AUDIO** recording for many types of TV and radio programmes, especially those set in a **STUDIO.** The performers are rehearsed in sections, often out of sequence with the programme order. In TV, the cameras also rehearse their **SHOTS,** and in audio the sound technicians **BALANCE** the **MICROPHONES.** Each section is then recorded as soon as possible after the rehearsal. Other methods that are not rehearse/record include rehearsing the show in the morning and afternoon, and then recording the whole show in front of an **AUDIENCE** in the evening. This is popular with comedy and entertainment shows.

RELEASE FORM   A form produced by a media **PRODUCTION** company that a **CONTRIBUTOR** to any form of **AUDIO** or visual recording is asked to sign. It shows that the contributor has agreed to take part in the recording. It releases the company from any subsequent obligation to pay for further exploitation of the product. All contributors who agree to appear in any production that is going to be sold to the public, broadcast or put on a website or shown outside a private collection, should be asked to sign a release form. The form should cover all known rights in the universe and any subsequent use of the contribution in any form whatsoever throughout the world and for eternity. The form may involve a payment or the contribution may be given free. It should only be used for members of the public contributing to a media product, and not for actors or other professionals, who will have a **CONTRACT**.

RENDER   Process used in computer video **EDITING** to create **DIGITAL** pictures and **SOUND** of the same high **QUALITY** as the **RUSHES**. The software builds video files and video effects as one complete sequence. This is the final process after all the decisions have been made during an edit on a computer-based editing system, such as **AVID** or **ADOBE PREMIERE**. Whole sections of a programme can be rendered separately or just a few selected frames. It usually takes some time to render a whole programme. **DISSOLVES** and **WIPES**, and other effects on some systems, have to be rendered as you go along, in order to see the effect. When the pictures and sound have been rendered they can be laid back to **VIDEOTAPE**, **CD** or **HARD DISK**. *See Offline Edit, Online Edit.*

REPORTER   Journalist working on **LOCATION** to view and reinterpret events for a print publication, TV or radio programme. A reporter will be expected to produce regular **NEWS** reports or comment on a topical event, as well as do on-the-spot **INTERVIEWS**. A reporter's main job is to get all the facts right and be totally accurate. This will entail double-checking names, statistics and information passed on by other sources. The job also involves some degree of interpretation of events to make sure the reader, listener or viewer can understand them in an interesting way. *See Presenter.*

RESEARCHER   Important member of the **PRODUCTION** team in any factual programme for radio or TV. Supports the **PRODUCER** and/or the **DIRECTOR** in making ideas happen. Has skills in several areas: is well organised, practical, good at lateral thinking, writes fluently, has excellent communication skills and is brimming over with ideas. The job includes finding out and checking facts, finding and selecting relevant music, finding and acquiring programme items and prizes, or finding and evaluating **CONTRIBUTORS** for a programme. Some researchers specialise in looking for and getting clearance for suitable **CLIPS** from film and video **ARCHIVES**. Others specialise in finding suitable members for an **AUDIENCE** show. Can also be the most junior member of the team. The term can mean someone who is there to help with absolutely everything in the show, but he or she will acquire relevant industry skills.

RESIDUALS   Payments in the form of **ROYALTIES**, paid to key personnel on a media production when a programme is sold abroad or repeated. People who may get residuals include writers, musicians, the **DIRECTOR**, the **PRODUCER**, and sometimes actors and performers, if it is in their CONTRACT. As the global market for media products expands, the question of residuals needs to be sorted out at the contract stage.

RESOLUTION   The clarity, depth of colour, fineness of detail and sharpness of a video or print picture. Resolution is measured in a variety of ways. For DIGITAL pictures, the greater the number of PIXELS in a digital camera equates with higher-QUALITY images and higher resolution. A camera may have more than five million pixels to produce top-quality images, but for prints, the PRINTER has to be able to read such fine detail. For ANALOGUE pictures, resolution is measured in lines on the TV screen: a PAL picture has 625 lines, while an NTSC picture has 525 lines. The overall resolution of any visual system, and therefore the quality of the final image, depends on how every element in the technical chain performs, from LENS to television receiver or printer.

RESOURCES   Refers to the technical and construction costs, with associated CREW, of a media product. Basically means enough finance to buy/hire the necessary kit and operatives to realise a SCRIPT and produce a moving-image or AUDIO product. Resources covers everything from the renting of a fully equipped TV STUDIO, to the hire of an underwater camera, or even the use of a church hall for rehearsing a radio programme. Everything except PRODUCTION personnel that is needed to make a media product comes under resources, and this is necessarily a large section in any moving-image BUDGET.

REVERB   Reverberation. The slow decay of reflected SOUND. Wherever sound is produced, it is reflected from all the untreated surfaces in the room, concert hall, church, theatre or STUDIO. In a large cathedral, a chord from the organ will be heard to reverberate several seconds after the sound has been created. Reverb can be unwanted, such as when recording an INTERVIEW, but reverb can be captured by a MIC and give presence and atmosphere to a recording. If the location is in an empty room, where the sound bounces off the bare walls, a recorded interview will sound 'boomy', with some echo. Recording in a bathroom has a similar effect. This makes it very difficult to listen to and is very unprofessional. However, for a singer, some reverb is often beneficial and can enhance the sound. For a drama recording in a sound studio, where a particular effect is required, reverb can be created electronically. This can give the impression that an actor's voice is coming from inside a cavern or high up in the dome of a cathedral. *See Sound Mixing Desk.*

REVERSE QUESTIONS   Doing a television INTERVIEW on LOCATION normally requires only one camera. This is for maximum flexibility, to save money and cut down on kit and personnel. How, then, do you film the PRESENTER asking the questions? This is done after the interview has taken place, by setting up reverse questions. These are pictures of the presenter asking the exact questions asked in the interview, as if to the CONTRIBUTOR, but without the contributor being present. So called because the presenter must make sure he or she looks to camera in the opposite or reverse direction to the contributor. So if the contributor is looking CAMERA RIGHT, then the presenter must look CAMERA LEFT. *See Shot Size.*

RGB   Stands for the three primary colours: red, green and blue. These are the three colours used to create a colour image in camcorders, video recording, PLAYBACK and TRANSMISSION systems. *See NTSC, PAL, Resolution, Widescreen.*

RIFLE MIC   *See Gun Mic.*

RIG   Both a noun, the rig, and a verb, to rig. To set up recording equipment, performance lights and SOUND systems, normally for an OB. Any equipment that needs time to set up is part of the rig for a television show, film, radio programme or concert. *See Live.*

RIP   Multimedia. The process of transferring music or other AUDIO material from a CD to a computer's HARD DRIVE is known as ripping. To rip a CD is, therefore, to copy it DIGITALLY, with no loss of QUALITY, onto a computer.

RISK ASSESSMENT   The process of assessing the nature, likelihood and possible severity of the risk of injury involved in making a media product. This is especially important on LOCATION, where personnel and equipment are involved. This can be anything from a car chase sequence – severe risk – to doing an INTERVIEW in an office, where the risk of injury to PRODUCTION and CREW is negligible. *See Hazard Risk Assessment.*

ROLLING NEWS   A NEWS-only broadcasting channel on radio or TV that recycles and updates its NEWS BULLETINS at regular intervals 24 hours a day. The news appears to be seamless. *See Newsreader, Presenter.*

ROSTRUM CAMERA   Moving-image camera, mounted on an overhead device, to look directly down onto a rotatable platform. Used for recording photographs, illustrations, artwork, models and other material onto VIDEOTAPE or film. A sophisticated rostrum camera

Rostrum camera

has motion control. Here, the camera is held on an overhead mounting above a motorised moving platform. A computer is programmed to control the way the platform moves and the zoom of the camera. This can film rotating pictures, zoom in and zoom out of small details, and affect a variety of fast and slow horizontal and vertical movements to make still pictures more interesting. These movements can be timed to coincide with the COMMENTARY or with music.

ROT   Recording Off Transmission. Sometimes it is necessary to make a recording of a radio or TV programme directly off air, especially a LIVE show. This is known as a ROT of the programme.

ROUGH CUT   The first edited version of a film, TV or radio programme with sequences in the desired order, but generally overlong and loose. *See Assembly, Editing, Fine Cut.*

ROYALTIES   Payments made to actors, performers, PRESENTERS, writers and musicians when a radio or TV programme is repeated or sold abroad, depending on CONTRACT. Many contracts allow for one repeat at an agreed percentage of the original fee. Royalties for other repeats, or repackaging for different channels and markets abroad, may have to be renegotiated. In publishing, royalties are paid to the author(s) of a work for each copy sold. *See Copyright, Residuals.*

RPM   Revolutions Per Minute. Refers to the number of times a record or disc on a turntable, or other device, revolves in one minute. A 12-inch vinyl record normally runs at 33⅓rpm. A 7-inch single revolves at 45rpm.

RTS   Royal Television Society, 100 Grays Inn Road, London WC1X 8AL www.rts.org.uk Important organisation in promoting and developing the art and science of TV in the UK. Organises annual awards ceremony for outstanding broadcast television programmes and technical achievements in several categories. Encourages student programme-makers with a prestigious awards scheme. Runs meetings, lectures, workshops and conferences about the television industry and broadcasting, in London and around the country.

RUNNER   Most junior member of the PRODUCTION team on a film or TV shoot. Can be asked to do anything that involves fetching and carrying or just helping, but should not have to make the tea *all* the time. This is a first job in the industry and should involve some learning experiences. Essential requirements include a good understanding of film and TV, a flexible approach to work, stamina, punctuality and the ability to learn quickly. *See Researcher.*

RUNNING ORDER   Document that gives the details of every ITEM and the correct order in which they are to be broadcast in a radio or TV programme. Essential for a LIVE or 'as live' show. The running order includes the source of each item – tape, STUDIO, CD, or OB – and other details, such as DURATION and who is presenting the item. Anything from a wedding to a children's day out could have a list of events put down in the order in which they should happen. It is essential for a broadcast media product that the order of items is known by everyone in the team involved in getting any programme on air. *See Camera Script, Schedule, Shooting Script.*

RUNNING STORY   NEWS or topical story for radio or TV that develops, or runs, over days, weeks or even months. Could be a murder investigation, a political upheaval or any story that will interest an AUDIENCE. A well-organised news room will keep its audience up to date on running stories and not let a story die. *See News Bulletin.*

RUN THROUGH   Refers to going through a whole TV or radio programme or show from beginning to end, before TRANSMISSION. Aim is to sort out any problems and review the material. Programmes created in a radio or TV STUDIO are complex to make, involving sophisticated technical resources and split-second timing. A run-through is essential.

a) MAGAZINE PROGRAMMES with a number of different ITEMS and a variety of complex technical RESOURCES are often LIVE, or recorded 'as live'. The run-through happens after any REHEARSAL and before recording. It is a way of going through the whole show, seeing all the items, both taped and live, so that ON-SCREEN performers, PRODUCTION personnel and technical CREW are fully informed as to how the show will come together. It is also essential in getting a correct timing for the show. If the run-through reveals the show is too long, then something has to be cut.

b) Can also mean a complete cast rehearsal of a drama or any TV or radio show, before it goes onto the set or into the studio for recording.

RUSHES   All the film or video FOOTAGE shot each day is known as that day's rushes. In the US, they are called DAILIES. The term comes from the early days of cinema when the footage SHOT each day was rushed to the LABS for processing overnight so that it could be viewed early the next day before shooting began. This is still how it is done on feature films. For TV production, the term rushes is still useful as a way of referring to original video footage before it has been edited. *See Editing, Film Stock.*

RV   Rendezvous. French for a meeting. RV is used throughout the industry to denote the LOCATION, such as a hotel, pub or car park where cast, PRODUCTION and CREW will meet up before going on a shoot, or doing any form of recording. It can be the actual location of the shoot. The RV is indicated on the CALL SHEET for each day. *See Schedule.*

SACD   Super Audio Compact Disc. New, very high-quality AUDIO disc FORMAT. Creates audio that can be played on a DVD player and benefit from the SURROUND SOUND cinema-style audio playback.

SADiE   Trade name for a DIGITAL computer AUDIO editing system, used in making radio programmes and for digital POST-PRODUCTION. *See Cool Edit Pro, Digital Editing.*

SAFETY ASSESSMENT   *See Hazard Risk Assessment.*

SAMPLING RATIOS   Way of indicating the RESOLUTION of the digital SAMPLING process used in video CAMERA, DIGITAL EDITING and POST-PRODUCTION. Written as three numbers, separated by colons, it is a way of measuring the ratio between the colour and the brightness, e.g. at the smaller, but still good-QUALITY, end is 4:1:1, used by Panasonic DVCPRO systems. DIGITAL BETACAM uses 4:2:2, a higher resolution used by top-quality broadcast systems. *See Audio Sampling.*

SCANNER   TV. The mobile CONTROL ROOM vehicle of a MULTI-CAMERA shoot on an OB. The scanner is the epicentre of the OB and is in two-way communication with the technical CREW, cameras, SOUND sources and PRESENTERS, and can make high-quality recordings or send video signals back to base.
  Multimedia. A scanner converts artwork, text or pictures into DIGITAL data that a computer can store and access. A typical scanner has a flat surface on which may be placed photographs, artwork or pages from books etc. This is known as a flatbed scanner. In a typical flatbed scanner, a CCD travels across, i.e. scans, the artwork or text and converts the information into digital data. A film scanner can convert a celluloid NEGATIVE or film strip into digital data. A transparency adaptor can be used to scan photographic slides and film negatives. RESOLUTION is important and is measured in dots per inch (dpi). A typical resolution is 600×1200dpi. Higher quality is 1200×2400dpi. For high-quality colour photographs, good colour depth is important. This is the amount of colours the scanner can record. It is typically between 24- and 36-bit. Colour is split up into RGB, red, green and blue. 24-bit records 8-bits for each colour, each with 256 shades from black to white. 36-bit offers even more colours and a huge tonal range for superb results.

SCENE   TV, film. A way of dividing up a SCREENPLAY into manageable parts that are related by time and LOCATION. For a moving-image production, a scene indicates the general area the camera needs to be in to shoot the scene. It does not show details of SHOT SIZE or camera ANGLES. A scene can contain only visual information, e.g. EXTERIOR shot of getaway car, screaming around a corner and disappearing into the distance; or it can contain dramatic DIALOGUE between the main characters in the film. In other words, a scene is what can be SHOT in one place, at one time, without involving a major resetting of the camera, set or lighting. Term is taken from the theatre to indicate that the ACTION takes place in the same time and setting. A scene in a stage play is generally much longer than a scene from a screenplay.

SCHEDULES   A media product almost certainly has a DEADLINE and, therefore, a schedule is needed to show what needs to be done by when. Schedules vary, depending on the scale of the PRODUCTION and the product. An overall television programme schedule would start with day one when the team assembles, would fill up with filming and editing dates, and end with final TRANSMISSION. This type of schedule will show what has to be done before going on to the next stage, e.g. you need to shoot your RUSHES before you can start EDITING. A modest TV programme will need a filming schedule, which shows what is going to be filmed where and when, and who is needed. A daily film schedule shows the sequence of events and details of time, place and personnel for a day's filming. ***See Call Sheet, Screenplay, Shooting Script, Shot List.***

SCREENPLAY   A SCRIPT that is written for a FEATURE film or TV drama. A screenplay may be an adaptation for the screen of a book or stage play or be totally original. It will have, typically, a beginning, middle and end, and FOCUS on telling the story visually and through the ACTION, with lively, realistic DIALOGUE. There is a standard way of setting out a screenplay for a movie. It should use a standard FONT size and LAYOUT. The aim is to create a story that can be interpreted creatively by the film's DIRECTOR.

SCRIM   A translucent screen in front of a lamp, e.g. a REDHEAD, to reduce its intensity and create a SOFTer light. Can be a built-in metal-gauze mesh on a studio LUMINAIRE or heat-resistant tissue paper pegged in front of the BARN DOORS of a lamp to diffuse the light.

SCRIPT   The essential working document that is the starting point for a film, TV or radio programme. Contains the DIALOGUE, which can be the words of a performer or an interaction between two or more characters in a drama. A radio script will contain all the LINKS and CUE SHEET material for any INSERTS in the programme, as well as details of music and guests. For a TV DOCUMENTARY or FACTUAL PROGRAMME, the script is revised to become a SHOOTING SCRIPT. This realises the words onto the screen, containing as much information as the DIRECTOR needs to shoot the programme. This may include camera ANGLES, SHOT SIZES, shot numbers, notes for performers, instructions for SOUND and the inclusion of all the other elements that will make up the programme. A script for a programme being made in a TV STUDIO is known as a CAMERA SCRIPT. The script for a feature film is generally called a SCREENPLAY.

SEARCH ENGINE   Multimedia. Website that searches for lists of other websites using a keyword system. Type in a keyword, e.g. 'Beatles', to a sophisticated and fast search engine such as www.google.co.uk or www.yahoo.co.uk. Within seconds, the DOMAINS of hundreds of web pages will be listed. Google suggested, in less than one second, 2,140,000 pages incorporating the word Beatles. Not all of them will be relevant, but the search engine prioritises the major websites at the beginning of the list. The user can then select and access the sites that seem most useful. Advanced searches are available. Because of how the system works, it is important to type in only essential words and try variations for best results. Word order matters, as search engines prioritise the first word. Avoid using 'and' or 'the'. Typing in a + before a word ensures that only web pages with that word will be listed. Different search engines find different results. It is worth asking for the same search in at least two search engines.

SECAM   Séquential Couleur Avec Memoire. Colour television standard TRANSMISSION system in France, Russia and some eastern European countries, and the former French colonies, such as Martinique. *See PAL, NTSC.*

SECS   Seconds. Used in radio and TV SCRIPTS to denote DURATION of an item, e.g. 40 secs. Also written 40″.

SEGUE   Musical term. Means to follow on. Pronounced 'segway'. Used in radio to describe how one disc or ITEM follows immediately after another, with no break. Used in a radio SCRIPT to indicate how an item should flow seamlessly into the next part of the show.

SELF-OP STUDIO   A radio STUDIO designed to be operated entirely by one person sitting at the MICROPHONE. Can be a small soundproof room, with just a microphone, a tape

Self-op radio studio

recorder or computer recording system and a couple of controls. This can be used for recording a **VOICE PIECE** or an **INTERVIEW**, such as an **INSERT** into a **NEWS** programme. A more sophisticated self-op studio can be found at most radio stations. It will be equipped with a multi-channel **SOUND MIXING DESK**, have telephone feeds, **CD** players, **MINIDISC** players, a computer and several mics. The programme **PRESENTER** or DJ will be able to go **LIVE** on air, and will operate all the equipment.

SEPMAG   Film. Means separate magnetic **SOUND**. Refers to the normal way sound is recorded when working with film. The sound is recorded onto a separate recording system, such as **DAT** tape. It is not recorded onto a magnetic **TRACK** that is combined with the celluloid film – an older system called **COMMAG**. *See NAGRA*.

SERVER   Multimedia. A powerful, centralised computer with huge data storage capacity, which sends data to other computers. Websites are stored on web servers. **EMAIL** is stored on a mail server.

SHAREWARE   Multimedia. Software available on the internet that is occasionally totally free to users. Typically, it is free for a limited period, after which time a registration fee is required. Useful source of inexpensive computer software programs.

SHOCKWAVE   Multimedia. Popular brand of software that allows the computer to read animated **GRAPHICS** and video. Can be downloaded from its website address, www.macromedia.com.

SHOOTING RATIO   Ratio of the quantity of film or video shot as **RUSHES** to the **DURATION** of the finished edited programme. This is measured by time expressed in minutes, or length of film expressed in feet. For a programme with a final edited duration of ten minutes, and with 100 minutes of video rushes shot, the shooting ratio is 10:1. This ratio becomes more important when shooting on film, as processing costs must be added into the **BUDGET**. The higher the shooting ratio, the more expensive the programme. This is less true of shooting on video, because videotape costs less than **FILM STOCK**, but the more you shoot, the more time it takes to view the rushes, and to edit. Also, it can take more time to acquire the **FOOTAGE**, unless the shooting ratio is kept under control.

SHOOTING SCHEDULE   A schedule devised by the **DIRECTOR** that is a detailed timetable of everything that is going to be shot for each day's filming. It can include details of **SHOT SIZE**, camera **ANGLES** and the way in which a subject is to be filmed, as well as details of **LOCATION**, time of day and technical requirements. The **CAMERAMAN** and other members of the **CREW** will base their filming day around the details in the shooting schedule. *See Call Sheet, Schedule, Shooting Script, Location, RV.*

SHOOTING SCRIPT   Outlines the structure of a television programme or film and includes all the essential elements that have to be filmed. Turns research results into a script **FORMAT** that can be used during shooting, so that everyone knows what the **PRODUCTION** team are aiming to do. No set format, but should be comprehensive, flexible and completed before principal filming begins. Will be sent to main members of the team involved in shooting, especially the **LIGHTING CAMERAMAN**, sound recordist and **EDITOR**. Typically, in a factual programme, includes: details of the mood and intended visual style of the programme; detailed description of the opening sequence; full details of **CONTRIBUTORS**, and where and how they will be filmed; details of difficult or expensive **SHOTS**, e.g. use of **HELICOPTER**; notes on the **PRESENTER's** role; may include indicative **COMMENTARY** notes; should include suggestions for music and **GRAPHICS**, and suggestions of where any added material such as **ARCHIVE** film will be used, and ideas for the **CREDITS**. Must include careful instructions for shooting any sequences that may involve **POST-PRODUCTION** work that will be affected by the shooting, e.g. use of **BLUESCREEN** or **CGI** material.

SHOOT OFF   Applies to a camera that **FRAMES** up a shot with something unwanted in it. This may be part of the **STUDIO** wall or the background that is not part of the studio set in the **SHOT**. It may be that part of the set needs moving to cover this area, or the camera will have to find a way of framing the shot without showing the unwanted object. The camera is said to be 'shooting off the set'. *See Shot Size.*

SHORT   A short is officially a film or video that runs in its complete form for under 34 minutes. In practice, the term is flexible, but shorts are nearly always less than around 40 minutes. Popular with young filmmakers, as a way of making a film on a very limited budget that can be shown at festivals or on the internet. In the film business, it is generally considered that you will not be hired as a **DIRECTOR** for a **FEATURE FILM** unless you have directed a good short. *See Show Reel.*

SHOT   What the camera is recording at any one moment during filming. A shot can involve a **ZOOM** or **PAN** or other camera movement within a sequence, or may have no camera movement at all, but contain the **ACTION** within the **FRAME**. A shot can be defined in a variety of ways – by the camera **ANGLE** or by the movement of the camera, e.g. **TRACKING SHOT**, or the size of the shot, or from where the camera is placed, e.g. **OVERHEAD SHOT**. In a **CAMERA SCRIPT**, a shot is the smallest unit that makes up a sequence or **SCENE**. *See Framing, Two-Shot, Shot Size.*

SHOT LIST   List of **SHOTS** taken on **LOCATION**, usually by the **PA**, in the order in which they were acquired, including **DURATION**, details of which **TAKE**, size of shot, any technical difficulties and who is in the **FRAME**, e.g. **REPORTER**. A typical shot list entry could contain this information: Presenter John Adams PTC. Take 3 MCU John DUR: 45" OK.

SHOT SIZE   The size of the subject within the **FRAME** of a **SHOT**. It is very important in making any sort of moving-image product that the **DIRECTOR** chooses a suitable shot size that fits the frame naturally, and that can be edited together in a way that makes good visual sense. This allows for smooth **CONTINUITY**. Standard shot sizes are referred to by their abbreviations. A **CLOSE-UP** (CU) shows the person's face, with the bottom of the frame along the line of the shoulders, just below the knot of a tie. A big close-up (BCU) shows just the face, cutting off some of the forehead and part of the chin. A **VERY BIG CLOSE-UP** (VBCU) shows a part of the face, such as the mouth, or eyes, or even just one eye. This is popular with music video directors. A **MEDIUM CLOSE-UP** (MCU) is slightly wider than a CU. The bottom of the frame runs just under the line of the top pocket of a jacket – sometimes known as the top-pocket shot.

A **MEDIUM SHOT** or **MID-SHOT** (both **MS**) cuts off at the waist, whether the person is sitting down or standing up. A **MEDIUM LONG SHOT** (**MLS**) cuts off a standing or walking figure around the knees. A **LONG SHOT** (**LS**) shows the person in full length, with the feet clearly in frame. A **VERY LONG SHOT** (**VLS**) shows the person or people quite small in the frame, with more dominance given to the setting. *See Angle, Crane, Dolly.*

SHOW PRINT   Final edited version of a film, printed from the **NEGATIVE** with all the **DISSOLVES** and other optical effects. This is the version of the pictures that will be transmitted or shown on screen in the cinema. The show print only refers to the pictures. The **SOUNDTRACK** for the film is completed separately.

SHOW REEL   Selections from a film or television professional worker's body of work collected onto one roll of film or video. The usual **DURATION** is about five minutes. Many people working in television or film create an attractive and engaging show reel with selections of images from the productions they have worked on. This can then be shown to potential employers to illustrate the quality of their work.

SHUTTER   Camera. Device in a still or video camera that controls the length of time that light is allowed to pass through the **APERTURE** onto the film or **CCDs**. If the shutter speed is doubled, it lets in half the amount of light. Shutter speed determines the effect of movement by the subject. In photography, a fast shutter speed of $\frac{1}{500}$ of a second can freeze the **ACTION** at a horse race or of a bird taking flight from a tree. A slow shutter speed is useful for a static object, where **DEPTH OF FIELD** is required, such as a view of a church across countryside. Correct **EXPOSURE** for a subject is when the shutter speed and the aperture are in the right combination for the circumstances. Modern still and moving-image cameras have **AUTO-EXPOSURE** that computes this relationship. Many **CAMERA OPERATORS** prefer to adapt their own settings to suit the subject and the required result. This is sometimes known as **EXPOSURE** compensation.

SHUTTLE   Control found on **AUDIO** and video equipment that allows the operator to search for a point on the tape or disc by seeing or hearing the material at variable speeds. Usefully, the material can be accessed at a much faster speed than normal. *See Jog.*

SIG TUNE   Signature tune. The regular opening and closing music, rarely more than 30 seconds, of a radio programme. Carefully chosen to reflect the mood, tone and content of the forthcoming programme. Well-known sig tunes come from long-running radio series, e.g. *The Archers. See Credits, Titles.*

SINGLE SHOT   **SHOT** with only one person in the **FRAME**. *See Two-Shot.*

SKILLSET   103 Dean Street, London WIV 5RA www.skillset.org The national training organisation for the TV, radio, film, video, **ANIMATION** and **INTERACTIVE** media industry in the UK. Main role is to promote and improve training for the industry. Provides up-to-date and well-researched relevant information about all aspects of the media for people who work or who would like to work in the industry. Recognised by the government as the specialist voice of media training. Has set up a range of industry qualifications and professional standards.

Encourages and supports new talent entering the industry. Actively supports skills training for organisations and individuals. Publishes authoritative careers information and research. Researches employment and market trends.

SLANDER   Legal term meaning to defame a person by word of mouth. The law of defamation includes **LIBEL** and slander. TV, radio, film, print and the internet are permanent, according to the law. Defamatory statements spoken or written by these media are considered under libel, not slander. Defamatory words spoken on a radio programme are therefore considered under libel. Cases of slander are rarely seen in a media context.

SLO-MO   Colloquial term meaning slow motion. Refers to running **VIDEOTAPE** at a slower speed than normal so as to slow down the **ACTION** in the pictures. Used to show action replays from sporting fixtures or create moods and/or dramatic effects in a film. *See Editing, Freeze Frame.*

SmartMedia   Trade name for a portable memory system used in **DIGITAL CAMERAS** to store images. A good-**QUALITY** standard 6×4-inch picture with high **RESOLUTION** needs about half a **MEGABYTE** of memory with this system.

SMOKE MACHINE   A machine for creating smoke or fog effects on a TV or film set. To make swirls of smoke or fog, an electric device atomises oil to produce a very fine mist that **DIFFUSES** the film lights. Much used in horror films. For dry-ice effects at rock concerts or for a more dense smoke effect, carbon dioxide is used. *See Special Effects.*

SMPTE   Society of Motion Pictures and Television Engineers. Organisation of professional engineers who set television technical standards in the UK.

SMTP   Multimedia. Simple Mail transfer protocol. The standard protocol for exchanging **EMAIL**.

SOFT   A **SHOT** that is not totally **OUT OF FOCUS**, but is not showing a crisp, sharp image that is completely in **FOCUS**. A **CAMERAMAN** would call this shot soft. At times, a soft image can be how the **DIRECTOR** wants the **SCENE** to look. Some of the **INTERIOR** scenes in the excellent Robert Altman film *Gosford Park* were deliberately slightly soft, giving the effect of a nineteenth-century painting.

SOFT LIGHT   Diffused or reflected light. Used in programme-making as a **FILL LIGHT** or as a way of lighting a subject that creates a naturalistic look and does not cast shadows. Created by using a **GEL** or a **DIFFUSER**, such as **SCRIM**, that softens highlights and shadows. Soft lighting effects can also be created by using a **REFLECTOR** or **BOUNCE LIGHT**. The largest and cheapest soft light source is a slightly overcast sky – there are no highlights. *See Filter, Hard Light, Blonde, Redhead, HMI.*

SOFTWARE   Multimedia. Computer program that allows a user to operate the computer for a huge variety of activities. Each application that a computer is capable of is run by a specially created software program. Microsoft and Apple Macintosh are the largest suppliers of software for the most popular activities, such as word processing, playing video games, viewing websites or **DOWNLOADING** material from the internet.

SOUND In media, the experience of listening to selected, relevant and distinctive sound is the essential complementary experience to watching carefully composed images. The process of acquiring and recording high-**QUALITY** sound for use in radio, TV and film can be complex, and requires skill, experience and suitable equipment. For a modern **AUDIO**-visual product, the sound is recorded **DIGITALLY**. It may be recorded onto disc, tape, **HARD DRIVE**, **MINIDISC** or **VIDEOTAPE**. Sound is recorded by using a **MICROPHONE**. There are many types for different purposes, e.g. a different mic is used in a radio **STUDIO** than is used for recording on a TV **LOCATION**. On location, audio for TV is normally recorded by a sound recordist using a portable **SOUND MIXER** that feeds directly into the camcorder. The best quality is obtained by using a high-quality microphone that is not mounted on top of the camera. For film, diagetic sound is recorded onto a separate recorder, such as a hard disk **NAGRA**. For a major film or TV production, the sound recorded on location, and other audio elements such as music, are track layed to correspond with the pictures. These tracks are then remixed in a sound **DUB** for the final **SOUNDTRACK**. *See Atmos, Baffle, Buzz Track, Control Room, Dolby, Dub, Foley, Sound FX, Track Lay.*

SOUND BITE Concise extract of **AUDIO**, usually just a few words, used on radio or TV. Often taken from a speech or longer **INTERVIEW** with a well-known person or politician. Can be used in a **NEWS BULLETIN** or at the head of a programme, and neatly sums up a point of view or stance on a particular issue. Can also be used by a newspaper, often in a **HEADLINE**.

SOUND CARD Multimedia. Device that fits into the computer and enables the computer to process and play **AUDIO** so that it can be heard on headphones or **SPEAKERS**.

SOUND FX Sound Effects. Recorded **SOUND** that is not speech, used in radio, film and television. Can be the sound of anything from the buzzing of bees on a summer's day to the sound of a train going through a station. May be something specific like Concorde taking off. Can be a created sound that accompanies an image. Most **AUDIO** on a wildlife television programme is created afterwards, as it is difficult to get suitable sound effects of animals on **LOCATION**. For sound FX in a movie, a **FOLEY** sound operator creates a sound effect that is naturalistic but more dramatic than an effect recorded in real life. This may be a punch or a groan or gunfire. To create the sound of a cowboy punching another cowboy, a Foley operator will put on a boxing glove and hit a punchbag. Throughout the media, a variety of methods are used to match the sound effects to the pictures. **CDs** can be purchased with comprehensive sound FX, useful to programme-makers. On location, some sound FX are recorded separately from the **DIALOGUE** to keep the sound clean and give the **EDITOR** a discrete recording to add as required at the edit. *See Atmos, Buzz Track, Dub.*

SOUND MIXER Equipment for mixing **SOUND** sources, either **ON LOCATION** or in a **STUDIO**. Generally refers to a small portable unit used for location recording, with no more than 16 input channels. *See Sound Mixing Desk.*

SOUND MIXING DESK Large **AUDIO** mixing console located in a TV **STUDIO** sound **GALLERY**, recording studio, **POST-PRODUCTION** area or **DUBBING** studio. Typically has at

SQN portable sound mixer.

least 24 stereo channels and a MULTI-TRACK digital recorder that can record up to 120 tracks. Each sound source is plugged in to a FADER so that the sound engineer can create a pleasing sound BALANCE, suitable for the product. The OUTPUT of the desk is recorded on whichever FORMAT is available. For TV, this may be DAT, and for music it is likely to be a multi-track recorder. *See Dolby.*

SOUND SUPERVISOR   Experienced SOUND person who works in a TV STUDIO. In charge of setting up the MICROPHONES and operating the SOUND MIXING DESK. Has to BALANCE the sound sources to create a mix suitable for the particular TV show. Has a small team of one or more sound assistants who load and operate the sound equipment, such as CD player, DAT machine, tape decks and other equipment. Also, a sound CREW, who work on the TV STUDIO floor, operating the sound BOOM and setting up the mics for the show.

SOUNDTRACK   All the AUDIO elements that have been combined to make the final audio TRACK(S) in a moving-image production. A feature film for cinema release will have a complex DIGITAL soundtrack for the multi-speaker SURROUND SOUND systems used in cinemas and on DVD. The soundtrack will have been finalised in the sound DUB, where all the tracks with the DIALOGUE, music and SOUND FX will have been laid to correspond with the pictures. Creating a modern movie soundtrack is a complex process that, in many cases, has as much impact on the AUDIENCE as the pictures, e.g. Michael Nyman's music for *The Piano. **See Dolby, Foley.***

SOURCES

a) In a radio STUDIO or for a SOUND MIXING DESK, refers to where the SOUND comes from, e.g. mic 1 or CD or tape.

b) Journalists see a source as someone who can provide them with pertinent information. A primary source is someone who can provide direct relevant information, usually by meeting face to face, or on the phone. Famously, the primary source, Deep Throat, in the US Watergate scandal, met the journalists in an underground car park to give information about President Nixon's government. A secondary source is information from an indirect route, such as CLIPPINGS, magazines and periodicals, library or other published source that is not exclusive but still may be hard to find.

SPAM   Multimedia. Junk mail that comes through via EMAIL. Can be extremely annoying, but some software will filter the worst offenders.

SPARKS   Colloquial name for an electrician working with a film or TV PRODUCTION.

SPEAKER

a) Short for loudspeaker.

b) Someone who is going to speak on a subject for a radio or TV programme.

SPECIAL EFFECTS (SFX)   Originally a film term to mean any effect that was out of the normal and was created either by an optical effect or by adjusting the camera. Special effects do mean explosions, war-zone effects, artificial thunderstorms and programmed motion-control shots, e.g. as used in *Star Wars*. But, increasingly, SFX are computer-generated images (CGI) that are produced DIGITALLY and interweaved seamlessly with the LIVE ACTION in POST-PRODUCTION. It's not just fantasy feature films that use special effects. A major BBC TV series about dinosaurs combined models, live action and computer-generated animation (CGA) to produce astonishingly realistic SCENES of prehistory. ***See Animation, Chromakey, Sound FX.***

SPECIALLY COMPOSED MUSIC   Music that is written and performed for a particular television show or film. The music may do a specific job, such as introduce a programme as the TITLES and CREDITS music, or be used throughout the programme or film. Typically, the COPYRIGHT in the music is bought out by the programme, so that it can be used only for that show. The composer may receive ROYALTIES for repeats and overseas sales. ***See Production Music.***

SPLASH   In newspaper language, this is the HEADLINE for the main front-page story. TABLOID newspapers often use a one-word dramatic headline splash to attract the reader and stand out on a paper stall, e.g. the *Sun*'s famous xenophobic splash during the Falklands War, when the Argentinean ship the *Belgrano* was sunk: 'GOTCHA'.

SPLIT SCREEN   Film, TV. Refers to the way two picture sources can be put together by splitting the screen vertically or, occasionally, horizontally. An obvious use for this effect is to show in vision the two participants in a telephone call. This is achieved as an optical effect on film. On video, it is achieved by using DIGITAL video effects in DIGITAL EDITING. In a TV GALLERY, it is achieved by using a VISION MIXING console or in a POST-PRODUCTION editing suite.

SPOT   Lighting. To adjust a FOCUSABLE lamp, such as a REDHEAD, to give a narrow focused – i.e. spot – light, illuminating intensely a relatively small area. A film or TV STUDIO lamp with a FRESNEL LENS can be adjusted to produce a narrow light beam. *See Barn Doors, Flood, Reflector.*

SPOT SOUND FX   SOUND effects created on the spot by a skilled operator, at the precise moment – i.e. spot – they are required in the SCRIPT. Spot FX are popular in drama production. They can be created to fit in with the script and be included in a radio programme as the programme is being recorded.

STANDARDS CONVERSION   The technical process of converting the material on a VIDEOTAPE, recorded on one television TRANSMISSION standard, such as NTSC, to another system, such as PAL. The three different television systems used worldwide, PAL, NTSC and SECAM, are incompatible. The pictures recorded on one system cannot be copied or transmitted on another system, without going through a piece of equipment called a standards converter. *See Resolution.*

STEADICAM   A film or TV camera mounting system where the camera is attached to the operator via a harness. This allows the operator to move or run with the camera and shoot at

Steadicam

the same time. The benefits of the system are that there is virtually no **CAMERA** shake or side-to-side roll evident in the pictures from the camera. The operator **FRAMES** the **SCENE** using a small **MONITOR** at waist level, rather than a **VIEWFINDER** at eye level. Used extensively in feature films and television dramas for chase sequences and to follow the action where a camera **DOLLY** cannot go. Also seen on the touchline of a televised football match. *See Tracking Shot.*

STEENBECK   Trade name of a professional film **EDITING** table. Used extensively throughout the television industry when 16mm film was the main method of acquiring **LOCATION** footage. This was before the advent of broadcast-quality portable video cameras in the 1980s. Now it is rare to see the distinctive four or six film spool-size flat plates arranged either side of a small viewing screen at eye height for the **EDITOR** sitting at the table. Revolutionised **FILM EDITING** when it was first introduced. *See Digital Editing.*

STEREO SOUND   **AUDIO** recorded through stereo **MICROPHONES** as left and right **TRACKS**. When replayed and heard on two separated **SPEAKERS**, gives a spacious **SOUND** image. The effect of hearing stereo is that the sound has width and depth. Some sounds, such as certain instruments or voices, come from different directions within a three-dimensional area. Virtually all broadcast and satellite television programmes are transmitted in stereo, as are most national radio stations. *See Dolby, Nicam.*

STICK MIC   Hand-held **MICROPHONE**, typically used by a television **PRESENTER** on **LOCATION**. Can have a cable attached to the **SOUND MIXER**. Can be a **RADIO MIC**, with a short stubby aerial at the base. Used on radio for **VOX POPS**.

STILL (PICTURE)   TV. Refers to any printed picture or photograph that will be used in a television programme. Also refers to a selected **FRAME** from a moving-image sequence, from film or video, that can be manipulated electronically or printed.

Film. Refers to a still picture taken from a feature film and used for publicity purposes. *See Freeze Frame, Rostrum Camera.*

STING   Radio. Short music jingle used as aural punctuation on a music station. Can be used to signify **NEWS**, traffic information or other regular event on a radio station. Can be a short music sequence with attention-grabbing speech, used as a way of identifying a radio programme or a particular radio station. *See Sig Tune.*

STOCK   Unexposed film before it has been loaded into the camera. Various lengths of moving-image film stock are kept on rolls in separate film cans for each gauge, e.g. 35mm, and length. To ensure optimum colour **BALANCE**, film stock needs to be kept at a low temperature and is often stored in a refrigerator.

STOCK FOOTAGE   Film, video and still images that are kept in a commercial film library or **ARCHIVE**. Many companies in the US and Europe offer specialist collections of images, often in one area, such as wildlife, music, **NEWS**, medical, scientific or sport. Used by TV **RESEARCHERS**, advertisers, **MULTIMEDIA** producers and anyone working in the visual communications industry, to source images for their products. Images are available for a fee, on **CD-ROM**, video and film. Some collections can be purchased outright on disc. Most **CLIPS** need **COPYRIGHT** clearance, and the client pays for the transfer as well as a library fee. Many stock footage libraries are listed in the *Stock Footage Index*, available from the Publishing Factory Ltd, Macmillan House, 96 Kensington High Street, London W8 4SG www.stockfootageonline.com.

STOP DOWN   Film, TV, photography. To reduce the size of the **APERTURE** and decrease the amount of light entering the camera. A **CAMERAMAN** may find that if the sun suddenly comes out during a shoot, he has to close the aperture by a couple of stops to ensure that the subject is not overlit. *See Focus, Lens, Shutter.*

STOP-FRAME ANIMATION   Technique where detailed models are made of clay, or another material, and moved very slightly before each frame is recorded. The attention to detail is enormous to create the right look. A famous example of stop-frame animation is *Wallace and Gromit*. Many children's TV programmes, such as *Noddy*, are recorded in this way. Model **ANIMATION** can be mixed with computer-generated images (**CGI**) for more spectacular effects. *See CGA.*

STORYBOARD   **FRAME**-by-frame drawing of the visual storytelling elements for a film or TV **PRODUCTION**. A well-drawn, sophisticated storyboard depicts the visual style, suggested camera **ANGLES**, elements of the costume, some character analysis and **SHOT SIZE**, as well as showing how the story can be told visually. Similar to a cartoon strip, the lower part of each frame contains **DIALOGUE** and other **AUDIO** elements, and may give detailed instructions for the **CINEMATOGRAPHER**. *See Screenplay, Shooting Script.*

STRAPLINE   Line of text, or just one word, **SUPERIMPOSED** over a moving picture, normally to add extra information, such as the score of a tennis match or the name of a place. In a newspaper or magazine, a small headline set above a main headline. *See Name Super.*

STREAMING MEDIA   Multimedia. **AUDIO**-visual content, such as a video, that is created on a website. This is fed continuously via the internet, to be accessed by a user connecting to the website. To have good-quality video streaming needs a fast connection, such as **BROADBAND**.

STRIKE   Film, TV.
a) To remove an object that is part of the **PROPS** from a set because it is no longer necessary to the **SCENE**.
b) At the end of the shoot, to dismantle the entire set.

STUDIO   A soundproofed space, which is set up to record radio or television programmes or to shoot a film. Many studios in a broadcasting company like the BBC come fully equipped with **MICROPHONES**, cameras, lights, a fully equipped **SOUND** suite and a sophisticated control **GALLERY**. Radio studios are usually fully equipped for broadcasting. Some have only basic recording equipment and cannot go **ON AIR**. Some studios are available for **DRY HIRE**, where the client brings in the required kit. Film studios, such as those at Ealing in London, are large closed spaces with a high ceiling, so that **LUMINAIRES** can be suspended over the set.

Some provide special facilities like a tank – a large space under the floor that can be filled with water for underwater filming. Also has facilities for making and storing sets. In California, large filmmaking companies, such as Universal, own huge studio complexes. These have several sound stages, and INTERIOR and EXTERIOR areas set up for making films, known as lots. *See TV Studio.*

STUDIO FLOOR   The area usually, but not always, at floor level of a TV STUDIO so that it is easy for scenery and equipment to be wheeled in and out. This is the performance area where the activity that is to go out LIVE, or be recorded, takes place within a set. It includes all the apparatus, such as cameras, MICROPHONES, sound BOOM and lights, as well as all the studio personnel required to make the programme. *See AFM, Floor Manager, Gallery, Pedestal, Props.*

STYLE   The particular way in which a print publication, radio or TV programme delivers its message. This may be evident by a visual style that has exciting camerawork, fast EDITING and striking GRAPHICS, or it may depend on the PRESENTER's style and the concept of the show. A well-known, experienced broadcaster could bring a certain style to a consumer programme. Its stylish settings, distinguished graphics, expensively staged acts, and the show's host could dictate the style of an entertainment show. The style of a radio show is often set by the presenter, e.g. John Peel. The selection and presentation of the music are important too. The content, FORMAT and GENRE are taken into account when creating a programme's style. Print publications are particularly conscious of graphic style, LAYOUT and visual presentation as a way of distinguishing their product from those of their many competitors.

SUB   To sub a SCRIPT or manuscript is to check it for factual, spelling and grammatical errors. In newspapers and magazines, a sub is a sub-editor, who edits and checks ARTICLES and writes headlines.

SUB-EDITOR   *See Sub.*

SUBTITLES   Film, TV. Translation of the DIALOGUE of a foreign-language film SUPERIMPOSED in text form onto the lower third of the screen. In television, subtitles are added to programmes to give viewers, who may have hearing difficulties, a visual way of understanding the dialogue. They are usually accessed by pressing a button on the remote control. *See Letterbox.*

SUN GUN   TV, film. A battery-operated portable lamp. Used on LOCATION by a film CREW to light an object or person where no other power is available. *See Handbasher.*

SUPER   *See Superimpose.*

SUPERIMPOSE   TV, film. To introduce a new image or GRAPHICS source and overlay it onto an existing picture. Also known as super. The effect when one picture is overlaid on another can appear like a DISSOLVE that has stopped midway. Superimpositions can be effected in POST-PRODUCTION or by the VISION MIXER in a television GALLERY. Digital editing systems, such as AVID, can create a range of video effects, including different types of superimposition. *See Aston, Name Super.*

SURROUND SOUND   Audio. Cinema-style SOUND system for the home via DVD playback. Created by employing a specialist SOUNDTRACK, available on DVD, and a number of SPEAKERS for different sound FREQUENCIES. These are typically placed behind as well as in front of the listener and viewer.

SVCD   Super Video Compact Disc. Way of recording video onto a compact disc. Can burn up to 60 minutes of high-QUALITY video onto a recordable CD. *See VCD.*

SWITCHED TALKBACK   TALKBACK that can be heard only by the person it is switched to. This is usually the PRESENTER of a TV show in a STUDIO or on an OB. The idea is that the presenter will not be interrupted or put off in mid-speech by hearing all the instructions that go out to the CREW on the open talkback system. Also, the DIRECTOR can speak exclusively to the presenter. *See Floor Manager, Gallery, Sound, TV Studio.*

SYNC   Synchronous. Refers to the way SOUND and pictures in a moving-image product are synchronised to run together so that the movement of a character's lips matches exactly the speech on the AUDIO track. *See Sync Sound, Lip Sync.*

SYNC SOUND   SOUND that is recorded at the same time as the pictures and matches the lip movements of the contributors. Sound DIALOGUE recorded on a film or TV LOCATION is generally sync sound, but movies re-record the dialogue in a DUBBING suite. The SOUNDTRACK of a finished film or programme has to be synchronous with the pictures. *See Diagetic, In Sync, Out of Sync.*

TABLOID   Newspaper that is half the size of a **BROADSHEET** newspaper, approximately 30×40cm. Aims to be popular and populist, e.g. the *Sun* and *Daily Mirror*. Characterised by limited amount of hard **NEWS**, use of large **HEADLINES**, extensive sports section, which is mainly football and racing, and plenty of gossip. Famous for 'kiss and tell' stories. Tabloid newspapers are also known as red tops.

TAKE   Film, TV. Term for each consecutive attempt at filming or recording a **SHOT, SCENE** or **SEQUENCE**. For a feature film or TV drama, each take is numbered in order. The **PA** takes notes of whether the take was successful, or the reason why it was no good (**NG**). These notes and other remarks make up the **LOG SHEET**.

TALENT   Performers working in front of the camera. Includes **ANCHOR**, actor, **PRESENTER, REPORTER**, DJ, musician. All colloquially known as the talent. *See Contract.*

TALKBACK   In both radio and TV, talkback is two-way **AUDIO** communication between the **CONTROL ROOM** and the **STUDIO**. In TV, the studio **DIRECTOR** in the **GALLERY** communicates with the **FLOOR MANAGER** on the studio floor and with **CAMERA OPERATORS** and sound **CREW**. Open talkback can be heard by everyone in the studio area with headphones. **SWITCHED TALKBACK** allows the director to talk directly and only to the **PRESENTER**, via the presenter's **EARPIECE**.

TALKING HEAD   TV. A **CONTRIBUTOR** who has been **INTERVIEWED** with few or no **CUTAWAYS** or other visuals is known as a talking head. The video **EDITOR** can only use the standard interview **SHOTS** and is not able to break up the static shots of the subject with relevant shots of what he or she is talking about. Reverse shots of the **PRESENTER** asking questions may be used, but this still offers no relief from a talking head.

TAPE   Magnetic recording medium of various **FORMATS** and sizes. **VIDEOTAPE** has various widths. **AUDIO** tape is usually ¼ inch or 8mm. There are many sizes and types of tape for both **ANALOGUE** and **DIGITAL** recording, depending on which format is used. Audio for radio is now almost universally recorded digitally, onto **MINIDISC, DAT, CD** or **HARD DISK**. High-quality audio **CASSETTE** is still used. *See Nagra, Sound, Multi-Track Recording.*

TARGET AUDIENCE   The specific **AUDIENCE** that any media product is aimed at. This may be arrived at through research, use of audience listening or viewing figures, or focus groups set up by the broadcaster or an advertising agency. The target audience may be grouped by age, e.g. children or over-50s, or grouped by interest, e.g. people interested in antiques or popular music (*Top of the Pops*). Radio stations target their audience by the type of music they play, e.g. Capital Gold plays golden oldies, or by genre, e.g. NEWS. DIGITAL TV channels tend to target their audience by content, e.g. Sky Sports.

TASTE AND DECENCY   Broadcasters are obliged to be careful not to 'offend against good taste and decency', but this can be difficult to define. Broadcasters have to comply with the law and with a code of broadcasting standards, laid down by the ITC for commercial broadcasters in the UK. The BBC is regulated by the law and its governors, who enforce standards of taste and decency. The BBC's code is enshrined in the PRODUCERS' guidelines, issued to all radio and TV producers working on programmes for the corporation. This includes guidance on the use of strong language and the scheduling of programmes with SCENES of an explicit sexual nature. These are controversial areas, as attitudes to sex and strong language change relatively quickly in the modern multi-channel era. Broadcasters are required not to cause widespread offence. Areas of taste and decency include sensitive attitudes to the victims of crime or natural disasters, and an agreement not to intrude into private grief and mourning. Whenever a programme contains material that might be offensive to some viewers or listeners, a broadcaster should issue a warning. Terrestrial broadcasters in the UK agree to abide by the 2100hrs WATERSHED.

TELECINE   Equipment that enables 35mm or 16mm film to be shown on television. The film is projected through a device that electronically scans the picture so that it can be recorded onto VIDEOTAPE.

TELEPHOTO LENS   Camera lens with a long FOCAL LENGTH that is rather like looking through a telescope in that it foreshortens the image and compresses perspective. A ZOOM lens works as a telephoto lens when you zoom in on the subject. Providing the FOCUS is set up on the zoomed-in angle of the subject, a zoom can be employed in vision to go from a WIDE ANGLE to a CLOSE-UP or vice versa. Can be used creatively for making INTERVIEWEES stand out from a fuzzy background, using the telephoto end of the LENS. Also useful for isolating subjects against a background or in a crowd. Used extensively in sport. *See Shot Size.*

TELEPROMPTER   Device that allows a PRESENTER in a TV STUDIO to speak straight to the camera while reading the words from a screen in front of the camera LENS. Special computerised equipment is used to project the words of the SCRIPT on to this screen, which is transparent to the camera. An operator types the script into the computer's memory, and can adjust the speed with which the words appear on the screen, according to the pace of the presenter's delivery. This is the standard way for a presenter to talk directly to the viewer without having to memorise a large number of lines. Portable versions are available for use ON LOCATION. *See Autocue, Newsreader.*

TFT   Thin Film Transistor. A high-QUALITY colour display system, used mainly in computer screens. Generally offers better quality and sharpness for a laptop screen than a standard LCD screen. *See CCD, Plasma Display Monitor.*

THE KNOWLEDGE   Impressive database of over 17,500 companies and services, including over 10,200 film and television professionals operating in the British film, TV, commercial,

AUDIO and VIDEO production community. Known as the industry bible. This is the place to find a list of professional film CREWS, or to locate an individual in a particular job specification, such as a sound recordist. Lists companies that hire equipment or provide services and facilities for the media industry. Can be purchased in large and expensive book form or accessed by free registration on the internet where it becomes www.theknowledgeonline.com.

THREE-POINT LIGHTING   TV lighting. The basic way to light a person or people on a set is the three-point lighting plan. So called because it can be set up quickly using three lamps: KEY LIGHT, FILL LIGHT, BACK LIGHT. To light a typical INTERVIEW situation, of a subject sitting on a chair in a domestic setting, is not as straightforward as it might seem. The three-point method offers a fail-safe system. The idea is that the key light provides the main illumination for the subject. It is placed just to the right or left of the camera and a little higher, so that it does not shine into the eyes of the subject. The camera LENS will be lined up in the subject's EYELINE, and the INTERVIEWER will sit as close as possible and at the same height as the lens. It is important to make sure the subject looks as good as possible, with no shadows under the eyes and no hot spots. This is helped by the fill light: a soft, diffused light, placed on the other side of the camera to the key. Its job is to fill in any shadows on the face of the subject, and any darker areas elsewhere, and to reduce the contrast. The camera should then see a balanced, well-lit but not overlit subject. The third source of illumination is the back light. This is placed behind the subject and its job is to separate the subject from the background to give a three-dimensional look to the SCENE. In practice, this means that for an interview the back of the subject's head is lit discreetly. The intensity of the back light varies according to the subject; usually some DIFFUSION is necessary. If the subject is truly angelic, it is possible to create a dramatic halo effect by placing the back light directly behind the subject. The overall effect needs to be checked through the VIEWFINDER to make sure it looks as the DIRECTOR wants it. A certain visual effect may be required, such as a beam of light coming across the face of the INTERVIEWEE from one direction, to suggest a definite light source that is relevant to the interview, or a naturalistic look. *See Blonde, HMI, Redhead, Reflector.*

THREE-SHOT   SHOT with three people only in the FRAME. *See Shot Size.*

TILT UP/DOWN   To move the camera, which is mounted on a TRIPOD, in a vertical arc, up or down. *See Dolly, Pan, Tracking Shot, Elevate, Depress, Zoom.*

TIME-BASE CORRECTOR (TBC)   Electronic device to ensure pictures and SOUND from different equipment can be run together IN SYNC and have no timing inaccuracies.

TIME CODE (TC)   A way of giving a discrete number to each individual FRAME in a video recording. Looks like this 02: 35: 54: 20 The first number (02) represents hours, the second (35) minutes, the third (54) seconds, the fourth (20) frames. Video runs at 25 frames per second. Professional camcorders generate time code that can be customised by the operator. This means that the TC can be set each day to continue the numerical sequence from the last shoot. In order to identify each frame, no two TCs can be the same on any programme. TC is recorded by the camera onto the VIDEOTAPE, but out of vision. It can be viewed on a video

Three-shot

recorder or when **EDITING** on a computer with suitable video editing software. A camcorder may also be able to record **REAL TIME** time code, which means it runs according to the time of day. The **SMPTE** time code is the one most universally used. *See Burnt-in Time Code.*

TIMELINE   Visual reference showing video **TRACKS**, edit points and **AUDIO** tracks in a linear form along a time reference scale, as part of the **ON-SCREEN** display in a computer video-editing system. Can also show an indicative **FRAME** from the **CLIP** used and indicate **TRANSITIONS** and other video effects. Audio tracks on the timeline show ramps and overlays. Most desktop systems, such as **AVID** and **ADOBE PREMIERE**, use this easy-to-read system. Virtually all the **EDITING** can be done using the timeline.

TITLES   The opening introductory sequence of a TV programme or film, giving its name and other information. For TV, the titles aim to grab an **AUDIENCE** by offering a stylised taster of the forthcoming show with catchy **GRAPHICS**. Normally, no more than 30 seconds long for an average television programme. Typically comprises graphics with the name of the show, pictures of any celebrities and a **MONTAGE** of pictures that set up the content and **STYLE** of the show. These are cut to catchy **SPECIALLY COMPOSED MUSIC**. For a feature film, the titles sequence is normally much longer and includes names of the key actors and **PRODUCTION** personnel. Can be very stylish and sexy and may not be at the beginning, such as in a James Bond film. Can be more low key and informational for a movie such as *A Beautiful Mind*. Some **DIRECTORS** prefer to dispense with a title sequence altogether in order to keep the audience spellbound from the beginning. Notably, Robert Rodriguez, in making *Spy Kids 2* for a young audience, goes straight into the **ACTION** at the beginning and only has brief **CREDITS** at the end. Even then, the credits run **SPLIT SCREEN** alongside the child lead actors, magically singing like rock stars. For some audiences, titles and credits can be a hindrance to good storytelling time. *See **Sig Tune**.*

TK   Short for **TELECINE**.

TONE   Radio, TV. Constant high-pitched **SOUND** used as a test signal. Activated to line up the **AUDIO** in a radio **STUDIO** or on a camcorder or tape recorder. Typically, tone is lined up at four on a **PPM**. Audio line level is at 1000Hz.

TOP SHOT   Shot taken from overhead or above the performers, e.g. from a rooftop camera. *See **High-Angle Shot**.*

TRACK

a) Camera movement for a **PEDESTAL** camera in a **TV STUDIO**. The camera itself is moved forward – track in – or backwards – track out – by a **CAMERAMAN**.

b) **ON LOCATION**, a camera movement in any direction where the camera is mounted on a **DOLLY**. This runs on specially laid tracks, keeping the camera steady and running smoothly; much favoured by filmmakers.

c) In **EDITING** film and video, a track is usually an **AUDIO** track, but can be a video track. A **SOUNDTRACK** for a film will be a **MIX** of many audio tracks. In computer editing, audio tracks are visible on the **TIMELINE**. *See **Track Lay**.*

TRACKING SHOT   Shot taken from a camera **DOLLY** where the camera moves smoothly to left or right, or forwards or backwards. Often follows the movement of a character. A tracking shot can also be used to create a number of different dramatic effects, depending on the context. *See **Track**.*

TRACK LAY   Film. To arrange and edit **AUDIO** tracks in the right order so that the **SOUND** comes in at the right time and is **IN SYNC** with the pictures. When they have been laid, the audio tracks are ready to go to the sound **DUB** for the final **MIX**. Track laying is done physically for a film, as the various audio tracks are on different strips. Most audio track laying for video is done **DIGITALLY**, with a computer **AUDIO MIXER**.

TRAIL   Short radio or TV taster item that is broadcast in advance of **TRANSMISSION** of a programme. Aim is to whet the appetite of the **AUDIENCE** for the delights in store for them on that particular channel or radio station. A form of advertising.

TRAILER   A short, fast-cut film, shown in cinemas before the release of a feature film. Aim is to tempt the **AUDIENCE** with **CLIPS** of the most significant moments. Tends to use dramatic music and an intense **COMMENTARY** to make sure the audience return to the cinema to see the complete film.

TRANSCRIPTS   Relates to radio or TV **INTERVIEWS** that are more than a few minutes long and need to be seen as text on the page to be edited. An audio **CASSETTE** of the interview is sent to a person who specialises in word processing interviews from **AUDIO** tapes and will provide an accurate transcript of the whole interview. This makes it much easier to choose extracts from the best answers and 'cut and paste' them to make an **ASSEMBLY ORDER**. *See Editing.*

TRANSFERS   To copy original recorded material onto another **VIDEOTAPE** format. Typically, transfers are of **RUSHES** from **DV** or **DIGITAL BETACAM** to **VHS** for home viewing. Essential for doing a paper edit, and to create an **ASSEMBLY ORDER**. Needs **BURNT-IN TIME CODE** to see the **TIME CODE** on the VHS tapes.

TRANSITION   Change from one **SCENE** to the next via a visual effect executed in **EDITING**. The most common transition in video editing is a **CUT**. Most video-editing software offers a range of transitions, such as a **DISSOLVE** or various types of **WIPE**.

TRANSLUCENT   Lighting. Refers to a covering that is semi-transparent. It allows some light to come through. Often is a form of **DIFFUSER**.

TRANSMISSION   The actual process of broadcasting to an **AUDIENCE**. Means to have a radio or TV programme sent to a terrestrial transmitter, cable or satellite, and broadcast on a recognised radio or TV channel.

TREATMENT   Detailed outline of how a programme or film idea can be realised on the screen. Usually written by the **DIRECTOR** to explain in visual terms what the story will look like and how it is going to be presented to an **AUDIENCE**. A standard treatment for a TV programme is usually no more than a page long. It has essential information, grouped under headings such as **TITLE**, synopsis of the content and suggested televisual elements. A treatment for a feature film could be three to four pages, emphasising the key events and important **SCENES** in the film. A fuller version of a treatment, with a **SCRIPT**, becomes a proposal, which may be many pages in length, depending on the film. *See Screenplay.*

TRIMS   Film. Sections or trimmings from the **RUSHES** that are not used in the final programme or film. Some productions put a selection of trimmings together to make an **OUT-TAKES** roll.

TRIPOD   Three-legged camera mounting, essential for steady, professional-looking **SHOTS**. A large variety of portable tripods is available, some made of modern, lightweight material such as carbon fibre. For really steady shots, especially on a windy day, a professional heavy tripod is required. *See Hand-Held, Dolly, Pedestal, Steadicam.*

TURN OVER   Instruction used by **DIRECTOR** or first **AD** on a set to signal to the camera **CREW** to start recording. Originated in early days of film where the camera was turned over or cranked by hand.

TV PRODUCER   The head of the **PRODUCTION** team on a broadcast TV programme. May be **FREELANCE**, working as an **INDEPENDENT PRODUCER**, or may work on **CONTRACT** for a small production company, or may even be a staff employee of a national broadcaster. May make corporate videos, music videos, promotional material or programmes for broadcasting.

Initiates the idea for the programme or series and chooses the production team. Makes the final decisions on all the creative and financial aspects of the programme. Very hands-on. Works on all aspects of the show, from initial ideas, scripting, auditioning and selecting talent, to researching and shooting material, and POST-PRODUCTION. Will also be involved in press briefings, advance publicity and any follow-up work resulting from the transmission. Has responsibility for the show's BUDGET, HEALTH & SAFETY on LOCATION, compliance with TASTE AND DECENCY issues and COPYRIGHT. Responsible for all aspects of making the programme and meeting the broadcast deadline.

TV STUDIO   Soundproof space where television productions are recorded or transmitted LIVE. A major broadcaster, such as the BBC, will own a number of TV studios and equip them with complex lighting, SOUND and engineering, to enable a MULTI-CAMERA operation, giving maximum flexibility to host a large range of shows. A typical studio will have a large soundproofed flat floor area with a minimum of five cameras mounted on PEDESTALS, a vision and production control GALLERY, a sound CONTROL ROOM and RACKS, and a sophisticated lighting RIG. Support services, such as PROPS, make-up and dressing rooms, will be nearby. A smaller studio can be just a suitable soundproofed space with some film lighting, one or two cameras, and sound that may be set up for NEWS or a talk programme.

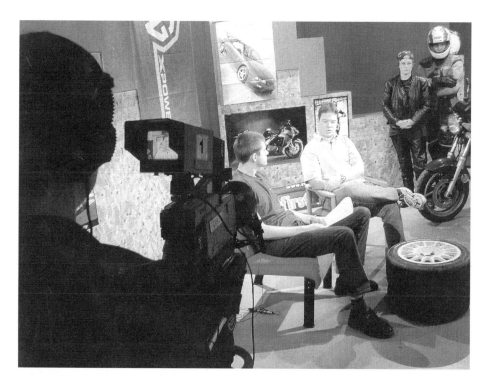

TV studio

TWO-SHOT A SHOT with just two people in the FRAME in equal prominence. A THREE-SHOT has three people, and so on. ***See Shot Size.***

TX TAPE Transmission tape. The TX tape is the best technical version of the programme and the one to be transmitted by the TV channel or radio station.

TYPEFACE Describes the look of the letters that make up the SCRIPT or text used in a newspaper or in GRAPHICS. There are many different designs, all with recognised names, such as Arial or Palatino. In a computer word-processing package, known as FONTS.

TYPOGRAPHY The way TYPEFACES are used in a print publication, newspaper or on the screen.

UHER Proprietary name for a portable, battery-operated professional **AUDIO** tape recorder. The Uher used to be the radio reporter's standard equipment for recording **INTERVIEWS** in the field. Has now been overtaken by **MINIDISC** or **DAT**.

UHF Ultra High Frequency. **ANALOGUE** TV channels transmitted in the frequency range of 300MHz to 3000MHz, and **DIGITAL** radio broadcasts.

UMATIC ¾-inch (19mm) **VIDEOTAPE** format, developed by Sony. Forerunner to **BETACAM** SP. There are two versions: **HI-BAND**, which is the better quality, and lo-band.

UNDERCOVER FILMING Filming without it being obvious that it is happening. Broadcasters have to make sure that filming undercover has some benefit to the public, such as the witnessing of a criminal act, or they could contravene privacy laws. Fixed cameras can be concealed behind two-way mirrors. Taking a camcorder into the street for discreet filming can be done by concealing the camera in an unobtrusive handbag or sports bag, with a special window. **SOUND** presents a more difficult challenge and involves a small **MICROPHONE** hidden in the **REPORTER**'s sleeve or concealed in an everyday object. Has to have sanction to go ahead from senior **EDITOR** in most broadcasting organisations.

UNDERCRANK Film term for operating a film camera at slower-than-normal speed. Goes back to the days when the film camera was operated by turning a crank or handle. The film goes through the **GATE** slower than normal. When projected at normal speed, it gives the effect, beloved of silent movies, of the action being speeded up.

UNDERRUN A radio or TV programme that is made too short for its allocated **DURATION** and has to have extra material added. The bad news may not be known until later, e.g. yesterday's **STUDIO** recording underran by 45 seconds.

UNDERWATER BLIMP Waterproof cover for a camera so that it can be used for underwater filming. These vary from a simple housing for a small **DV** camera, such as an EWA Marine underwater housing, which can go to a depth of five metres, to special heavy units for deep-sea diving.

UNIDIRECTIONAL MIC Type of **MICROPHONE** that picks up **SOUND** very largely from one particular direction only. Useful for cutting out background noise. Best example is a **GUN MIC**.

UPSTAGE   Way of describing how an actor should move or where an object should be placed in relation to the camera. Taken from the theatre, upstage is to go further away from the camera. DOWNSTAGE is to come nearer the camera.

URL   Internet. Unique Resource Locator. Technical name for a website address. Each and every website has one of these. *See World Wide Web*.

USB   Computer. Universal Serial Bus. Standard connection between a computer and a PERIPHERAL device, such as a PRINTER, SCANNER, DIGITAL CAMERA, personal organiser or external HARD DRIVE. Detects when a new peripheral has been connected and finds the software for it. Can link over 100 items, using a USB hub.

VCD Video Compact Disc. Up to 80 minutes of video that can be recorded onto a recordable CD. The QUALITY is about the same as average VHS, but low compared to SVCD. *See DVD.*

VCR Video Cassette Recorder. Any machine that records onto to a VIDEOTAPE cassette system, such as VHS, DV or DIGITAL BETACAM.

VERY BIG CLOSE-UP (VBCU) Shows a part of the face of a person, such as the mouth or an ear. Used more and more by STYLE-conscious DIRECTORS, particularly for music interviews. *See Shot Size.*

VERY LONG SHOT (VLS) Shows the person or people in full length and relatively small in the FRAME. More dominance given to the setting than to the subject(s). *See Shot Size.*

Very Long Shot (VLS)

VHF Very High Frequency. Domestic radio transmission FREQUENCY, also called FM, from 30 to 300MHz. Most radio stations are between 88 and 108MHz. Other VHF frequencies are used for communication systems by the police and the military.

VHS Video Home System. Consumer video-recording system, developed by JVC, using ½-inch magnetic tape CASSETTES. The main home video-recording system throughout the world. Gradually, may be superseded by DVD, but not until one DVD recording FORMAT has been agreed by the manufacturers.

VIDEOTAPE Magnetic particle tape that can record pictures and SOUND in a DIGITAL or ANALOGUE format. Usually encased in a plastic CASSETTE for protection and ease of use. *See Betacam SP, Digital Betacam, DV.*

VIEWFINDER TV. Miniature TV MONITOR, usually in black and white, mounted on a video camera, showing what the camera sees through the LENS. Allows the CAMERA OPERATOR to accurately FRAME the subject. Modern camcorders often have a flatscreen LCD colour monitor that pulls out of the side of the camera and can be used as a viewfinder. The viewfinder on a film camera does the same job of allowing the operator to see what the camera sees through the lens, but works through a system of mirrors.

VIRTUAL STUDIO A TV STUDIO that exists only as a picture on a computer. Using specialist software, a computer can create any desired environment into which real people can

TV studio camera viewfinder

be placed. When combined with **DIGITAL** video effects (**DVE**) a virtual picture can be **KEYED** onto blue backgrounds in a bare studio. A **NEWSREADER** or a **PRESENTER** appears to be reading the **NEWS** from the lush, three-dimensional environment of the computer-generated studio. This could be a space-age room, an old library or whatever the **DESIGNER** decides. This technique can be used to key moving pictures into a **BLUESCREEN** studio, where a presenter can appear to walk into dungeons and climb onto the battlements of a castle without leaving the studio. *See Chromakey*.

VIRUS   Computer. Nasty computer code that can have devastating effects on your computer, such as removing files and programs or even destroying the computer's **HARD DRIVE**.

VISION MIXER   Works in a **MULTI-CAMERA** TV studio **GALLERY** and operates the **VISION MIXING DESK**. The job requires less technical ability than an innate sense of timing and rhythm, and an ability to watch a large number of preview monitors at the same time and cut between sources with confidence and sensitivity. Although the **DIRECTOR** may call the **SHOTS** on a **LIVE** show, a successful result is often down to the consummate skills of the vision mixer who actually **CUTS** at precisely the right moment. During a live show or a recording, the main job is switching from one camera to another and between other visual sources. A modern **DIGITAL** panel has the possibility of a large number of visual effects, including picture manipulation, **FREEZE FRAME** and a bewildering variety of **MIXES**, **WIPES**, superimpositions and multi-screen effects. The vision mixer will know what can be done and how, but the director will specify what is required and when. A good vision mixer is a great asset, as he or she can really make a difference to the pace and timing of a programme. *See Superimpose.*

VISION MIXING DESK   A slightly ramped control console, fitted in the **GALLERY** of a TV **STUDIO**, consisting of push buttons in two or more banks and a master **FADER**. All vision sources come into the panel and can be previewed on a **MONITOR**. The panel also allows for **DIGITAL** video effects and **CHROMAKEY**. The controls on the panel allow the operator to select and manipulate chosen pictures from a large number of sources, according to the **SCRIPT** and requirements of the show being recorded or going out **LIVE**. The pictures are displayed on a bank of preview monitors behind the panel and the operator uses the panel to **CUT**, **MIX**, **FADE**, **WIPE** or use the **DVE** to create the desired effects. *See TV Studio, Talkback, Gallery.*

VOICE OF THE LISTENER & VIEWER (VLV)   Voice of the Listener & Viewer, 101 King's Drive, Gravesend, Kent DA12 5BQ Email: vlv@btinternet.com An independent association, funded by its members, democratically governed and with no political, sectarian or commercial affiliations. Founded as Voice of the Listener in 1983, by Jocelyn Hay. Realising that issues to do with radio and television were closely interlinked, the word 'Viewer' was added to the title in 1991. Represents consumer interests in broadcasting. The only organisation in the UK speaking for listeners and viewers on all broadcasting issues, including the structures, regulation, funding and institutions. Supports the principle of public service broadcasting. VLV works to keep listeners and viewers informed about current developments in British broadcasting, including proposed new legislation, public consultation on broadcasting

Small vision mixing desk

policy and the likely impact of digital technology. Produces a quarterly news bulletin, mailed free to members. Publishes regular reports and briefings on broadcasting developments, copies of its submissions and responses to public consultations, and edited transcripts of most of its public lectures, seminars and conferences. All are available from the VLV librarian. For details of student and academic membership, visit www.vlv.org.uk.

VOICE-OVER (VO)   A short, written SCRIPT that is read out of vision over relevant pictures in one or two sections of a TV programme or film. Often a short piece read by the REPORTER or PRESENTER over pictures to do with the story being recorded. Not quite the same as COMMENTARY, which is a written script read by a narrator and runs right through a programme, adding information and driving the story.

VOICE PIECE   Radio. A written SCRIPT, usually read by the author, in the form of a conversational talk to the listener, often on its own or as an ITEM in a MAGAZINE PROGRAMME. Probably the most famous voice piece on UK radio is that delivered each week by Alistair Cooke on BBC Radio 4, his 15-minute *Letter from America*.

VOLUME   The loudness of a SOUND signal. Technically, the sound pressure level produced by a loudspeaker. Can be adjusted on electronic equipment by the volume control, recognised by its universal ski-slope logo, which adjusts the gain on the loudspeaker AMPLIFIER.

VOX POPS   Radio and TV. Derives from the latin *vox populi*, and means voice of the people. Term for a collection of short statements recorded in the street in answer to a question about a controversial topic. The participants are shot in CLOSE-UP and cut together in a MONTAGE. Vox pops are not a representative or scientifically selected cross-section of the general public, but a useful way of sampling public opinion and setting up a discussion programme.

VPL   Video Performance Ltd, 1 Upper James Street, London W1R 1LB www.musicmall.co.uk Collects licence fees for the cable, satellite and terrestrial broadcasting of music videos. VPL offers advice on COPYRIGHT issues to do with music (pop) videos. *See Copyright, Music Copyright, MCPS, PPL, PRS.*

VT   VIDEOTAPE. *See DV, Betacam SP, Digital Betacam, Formats.*

VU METER   Volume Unit meter. Found on AUDIO equipment and calibrated in DECIBELS. Measures the strength of the signal. Useful as an indicator of the recording level of an audio signal from a MICROPHONE or other equipment. *See PPM.*

WALK-ON   A walk-on is basically an EXTRA in a TV drama or film who is given a specified function. Some walk-ons are given things to do, e.g. sell flowers, others may just feature for a few seconds in a SCENE. A walk-on is paid more than an extra. Can negotiate for further payment if asked to say a few words, in which case becomes a speaking walk-on.

WALKTHROUGH   Drama. Going through a SCENE with the actors saying their lines in a form of dress rehearsal, but usually without PROPS. There may be stops and discussion over lines, moves and how certain things can be achieved for the camera.

WALLPAPER   Colloquial term used in editing to describe any vaguely relevant pictures that can be put over INTERVIEWS or COMMENTARY, in order to give extra pictorial appeal to an otherwise rather visually dull interview.

WAP   Multimedia. Wireless Application Protocol. Standardises material from the internet into a simplified form, to make it readable by hand-held wireless devices such as mobile phones, pagers and two-way radios. Primarily used as a system that makes the internet available to mobile phones.

WARM-UP   The introduction that the AUDIENCE in a TV or radio recording receives prior to the show itself. Can be done by the PRODUCER but normally, and especially for any light entertainment show, there is a professional warm-up comedian, complete with newly minted topical jokes, to get the audience into the right frame of mind to laugh in the right places during the recording.

WATERSHED   Term given by the terrestrial TV broadcasting companies to the time when programming can be more suitable for an adult audience. This is, by consensus, 2100hrs each evening. Before that time, broadcasters follow a policy that all programmes should be suitable for a general audience, including children. Pre-watershed programmes should not include unsuitable scenes of sex, violence, bad language or distress. There is no watershed in radio, but care is taken not to SCHEDULE unsuitable programmes at those times of day when children may be listening, especially during the school holidays.

WATT   Unit of electrical power.

WAVELENGTH   The length of a cycle in a SOUND wave, expressed in metres. A radio station transmits on a particular wavelength, such as 194 metres.

WEB   Short for the WORLD WIDE WEB.

WEBCAM   Multimedia. Small, low-RESOLUTION camera, attached to a computer, which sends pictures via a website to other users on the internet. Webcams can be fitted anywhere, but need a cable to the computer and suitable software in order to stream pictures. More expensive versions are cable free. Some people like to have them positioned on the top of the PC, to send pictures of themselves to family and friends.

WEBSITE   Multimedia. Location for individual pages on the internet. *See World Wide Web.*

WHITE BALANCE   A way of making sure the colour of the pictures from a video camera accurately represents the true colours in a SCENE, by matching the COLOUR TEMPERATURE of the light source. Before shooting any scene on a camcorder, a white balance is required so that the camera can adjust to the temperature of the lighting of the scene, especially when moving from INTERIOR to EXTERIOR shooting. The camera looks at a white surface, e.g. sheet of paper placed where the subject will be in the SHOT, and, by pressing a button, will electronically adapt to the current lighting temperature.

WIDE ANGLE   A wide angle or WIDE SHOT covers all the ACTION in a SCENE in one SHOT and is taken with a WIDE-ANGLE LENS. The characters may be small in the FRAME and the lens will exaggerate the apparent distance between people or objects. The advantage is there is a lot more in the shot than a standard view and, as the name suggests, it covers a wide area, such as a landscape. A wide-angle lens used from close range can create images that have a lot of impact and attract the viewer's attention.

WIDE-ANGLE LENS   A camera LENS with a short FOCAL LENGTH, used for taking a WIDE SHOT.

WIDESCREEN   Terrestrial broadcast television in the UK is now broadcast predominantly in the widescreen FORMAT. The ASPECT RATIO has changed from the original cinema standard of 1.33:1, or, basically, 4:3, that was adopted by television TRANSMISSION systems throughout the world, to an aspect ratio of 16:9, known as WIDESCREEN. There are, however, many different versions of this, mainly because broadcasting channels do not want to restrict the viewing of most of the population, who have not yet changed to widescreen. Most films are now produced in a widescreen format. The width of the screen is between 1.85 to 2.4 times greater than the height. This means that for every centimetre of screen height, the visual part of the movie is between 1.85 to 2.4 times as wide. This results in a panoramic-type view. *See Anamorphic, Letterbox.*

WIDE SHOT   *See Wide Angle.*

WILDTRACK (W/T)   SOUND recording taken at the time of shooting on LOCATION that is not synchronous with any pictures. Recorded on the camcorder, the operator records COLOUR BARS to indicate there is a wildtrack sound recording and no useable pictures. Useful for recording a BUZZ TRACK or location music, which will later be used over pictures.

WINDSHIELD   A plastic foam cover that fits over the sensitive area of a MICROPHONE to protect it from wind noise when on LOCATION. Also used in radio and SOUND studios to stop the sibilant 'pop' noises that a **PRESENTER** is liable to make when talking with the mic positioned right in front of the mouth, where the air from the voice creates wind noise and 'POPS'. A sound recordist, on location with a film **CREW**, will typically use a large windshield that looks like a long hairy sock. This is a cylindrical plastic cover that holds the mic in a cradle inside and can be fitted to a **FISH POLE**, allowing the mic to be moved around, protected from wind noise, and noise from the cable and the mic itself moving. This can make a nasty clunking sound (mic rattle), often heard on live radio sports interviews.

Using a gun mic with windshield on location

WIND-UP　Means to come to the end of an **INTERVIEW** or other activity that is being recorded for radio or TV. Generally given in the form of a signal to the **PRESENTER** to indicate that the interview has gone on long enough and should end as soon as possible. Seen in a **TV STUDIO** as the signal by a **FLOOR MANAGER** to a **PRESENTER** or **ANCHOR**. Comprises the index finger forming a large circular winding movement that is initiated by an instruction from the studio **DIRECTOR**. In radio, the **PRODUCER**, particularly of a current affairs programme, will use the same signal to indicate through the glass of the **CONTROL ROOM** that the interview has run out of time and must end. More dramatic is the cut signal. This comprises the index finger being drawn across the neck to indicate a cut throat. This means, stop the interview now.

WIPE   A video **TRANSITION** where the incoming picture wipes away the picture already on the screen. There are a large variety of wipes, with names that generally reflect how they do the job, e.g. clock wipe brings in the new picture with a line similar to a clock hand that rotates clockwise round the **FRAME**; **IRIS** wipe starts as a small round **APERTURE**, or hole, that opens out to reveal the new picture. There are vertical and horizontal wipes, and ones that work like a pair of opening lift doors. Others dissect the screen diagonally. Most computer video-**EDITING** software has a collection of wipes under the transitions menu. A small icon diagrammatically describes the way each one works. In a TV studio **GALLERY**, the **VISION MIXER** is able to access a selection of wipes on the mixing panel to create a bridge between **SCENES** in a show or as visual punctuation.

WORKING TITLE   Temporary name given to a programme while it is in **PRODUCTION**. Sometimes becomes the actual title of the show. Tends to change when the team comes up with a really attractive, permanent title during production, or if the **EXECUTIVE PRODUCER** decides on some completely different title for **TRANSMISSION**.

WORLD WIDE WEB (www.)   Multimedia. That part of the internet that joins all the **WEBSITES** together. Gives its name to the domain prefix of a website: www.

WRAP
a) In moving-image **PRODUCTION**, the word wrap means only one thing – the end of filming for that day, as in, 'that's a wrap'. A final wrap means the end of shooting for the entire production.

b) In radio, a wrap is an **INTERVIEW** with some **ACTUALITY** material that is 'wrapped around' by a voice piece from the reporter at the beginning and at the end. Often found in current affairs programmes or breakfast shows.

WRITERS' GUILD OF GREAT BRITAIN   430 Edgware Road, London W2 1EH Email: tostia@wggb.demon.co.uk Society for all types of writers. Provides support for members on a huge variety of issues, including **COPYRIGHT** and payments. Has agreements with the main broadcasting companies, such as BBC, ITV and the independent producers' organisation, **PACT**.

WRITING FOR TELEVISION   There are a number of ways that anyone who is hoping to write a **SCRIPT** that would interest a TV **PRODUCER** can go about getting the script seen by the right person. If you are really serious, it is best to find an agent who will make sure your script gets to the right people. It is also very useful to join the Writers' Guild of Great Britain or the US equivalent. Most broadcasting channels have a **COMMISSIONING EDITOR** for each area or genre, such as comedy, drama or children's, whose job it is to find exciting new material for their channel. You can send your script direct to the relevant person. Do make sure that you have a presentable and original script that is carefully tailored to the specific channel, otherwise it will come back with a depressing rejection note and possibly very little explanation. More suggestions on script writing can be found in the handbook *Digital Television Production* (Arnold 2002).

XLR Professional AUDIO cable connection used for audio circuits. Has three channels: a left channel and a right channel for STEREO and a shielded ground. *See Microphone.*

ZERO LEVEL Refers to TONE that is at the standard test level of 1000Hz, used to LINE UP broadcasting equipment. *See Audio, Frequency, Sound.*

ZIP Multimedia. Compression system for computer files. Useful for moving files over the internet. Large files can be saved with this system using a PERIPHERAL known as a zip drive. Visit www.winzip.com.

ZOOM A LENS with a variable FOCAL LENGTH. Enables the CAMERA OPERATOR to FOCUS on subjects that are near, as well as subjects that are relatively far away, depending on the exact characteristics of the lens. Can be used in vision to zoom in on a subject or zoom out from a subject with the subjects in focus, providing the focus on the nearest subject has been set initially. Too much use of the zoom creates a push-me-pull-you effect that is not desirable in a professional television or film production.